EDITORIAL
Editor Maxwell Cooter
Art editor Bill Bagnall
Production editor Maggie Holland
Digital Production Manager Nicky Baker
Contributors Stuart Andrews, Mary Branscombe,
David Cartwright, Caroline Donnelly, Tom Gorham,
Dennis Howlett, Jane McCallion, Lesley Meall,
Davey Winder

MANAGEMENT
MagBook Publisher Dharmesh Mistry
Operations Director Robin Ryan
MD of Advertising Julian Lloyd-Evans
Newstrade Director David Barker
MD of Enterprise Martin Belson
Chief Operating Officer Brett Reynolds
Group Finance Director Ian Leggett
Chief Executive James Tye
Chairman Felix Dennis

MAGBOOK CloudPro

IT for small businesses: be successful without an IT
department ISBN 1-78106-225-0

The MagBook brand is a trademark of Dennis
Publishing Ltd. 30 Cleveland St, London W1T 4JD.
Company registered in England. All material © Dennis
Publishing Ltd, licensed by Felden 2013, and may not
be reproduced in whole or part without the consent of
the publishers.

LICENSING & SYNDICATION
To license this product please contact Carlotta
Serantoni on +44 (0) 20 79076550 or email
carlotta_serantoni@dennis.co.uk. To syndicate
content from this product please contact Anj Dosaj
Halai on +44(0) 20 7907 6132 or email anj_dosaj-
halai@dennis.co.uk

LIABILITY
While every care was taken during the production of
this MagBook, the publishers cannot be held
responsible for the accuracy of the information or any
consequence arising from it. Dennis Publishing takes
no responsibility for the companies advertising in this
MagBook.

The paper used within this MagBook is produced
from sustainable fibre, manufactured by mills with a
valid chain of custody.

Printed at Polestar Stones

Welcome

IF YOU'RE RUNNING a small business, you may worry spending money on IT equipment is not the best use of your cash. It all mounts up: the cost of kit and the price of software and technical support. The Federation of Small Businesses (FSB) is keen to drive uptake of technology as it knows the advantages.

According to a recent FSB survey, investment in IT will help SMBs grow faster and bigger. But, despite this, only around a third of small businesses have a real digital presence. This needs to change.

Large enterprises see IT as a way to drive up profits and add value. They have the benefit of dedicated IT teams to ensure that technology is being used efficiently. That option is not open to the smaller business but, thanks to the growing use of cloud technology, even small firms have the option of – and access to - greater computer power.

This is not a book for the sole trader surviving on one PC and Excel spreadsheets, but for any company employing people – or hoping to employ people. It's a book for companies looking to use IT constructively and gain a business advantage. It's a book for those small traders who look wistfully at the types of apps and services large enterprises can call on and want to know how they can benefit too. It's a book for firms who have a tiny bit of IT expertise but don't contain a whole server-room of techies.

If you want to run without an IT department, this book will provide some guidance about what to look for and what questions to ask. We hope you find it useful

Thanks for reading.

Max Cooter, Editor

INSIDE

MAGBOOK

IT FOR SMALL BUSINESSES
Be successful <u>without</u> an IT department

From the experts at **CloudPro** In association with **Sage**

TIPS AND TRICKS TO MAKE IT WORK FOR YOU
THE GUIDE TO HELPING SMALL BUSINESSES THINK BIG
SUCCESS WITHOUT TECH KNOW-HOW

ISBN 1-78104-025-0
www.magbooks.com

■ CHAPTER 1 GETTING STARTED

Let's start at the very beginning

Often the first steps in any new venture are the most daunting, but they set the foundation for what's to come so it's very important to get the basics right.

YOU RUN A SMALL business and wonder what life would be like if things ran more effectively. You've worked in large companies and have been envious of the type of resources that big corporations boast – the sort of sophisticated apps and computing power that are way beyond your budget and, more importantly, your levels of expertise.

One of the things that separates the average enterprise computer system from the small business one is the existence of an IT department. Most large organisations have one, usually located in the basement and populated by blokes (they're nearly always male) who wear jeans and t-shirts and will appear at your beck and call to fix broken machines or wonky software, usually tutting loudly. Alternatively, they appear from time to time making notes about every machine in the place and then scurry away back down to the confines of the basement.

There seems to be little way of penetrating this world. Indeed, it's one that seems as closed as the Freemasons. The IT department appears to have its own jargon, its own dress sense, and its own way of doing things. In essence, it has its own culture that seems at odds with the rest of the organisation.

Small businesses would love to call on expertise such as this, but, thus far, it's not been possible. And it's not just a question of more resources. The rich are different from you and me, said F Scott Fitzgerald, but he wasn't just speaking about the additional wealth, he was talking about a different mindset, a different way of working.

SETTING ASIDE DIFFERENCES

The difference between software that people use on their home and office PCs and the ones they use in the work environment lies in this interconnection. An individual sitting at his or her desk in the office has – just a click away – a vast amount of enterprise services.

Different companies have different software programs available for their users: these could range from some of the basic office productivity solutions such as email, word processing and collaboration tools, to the more advanced enterprise

> One of the things that separates the average enterprise computer system from the SMB is the existence of an IT department.

> There seems to be little way of penetrating this world. Indeed, it's one that seems as closed as the Freemasons.

software. This could include apps such as e-commerce software, enterprise resource planning (ERP), customer relationship management (CRM), human resources systems, project management, enterprise content management, business intelligence and a multitude of other such software and services.

One of the key features of enterprise software is that it's not delivered in a single form. It is highly customisable and can be tailored to your unique needs. And that's where the IT expertise comes in.

It's this sort of infrastructure that provides large organisations with the ability to handle business processes so adroitly. This means IT is not just a cash drain on a company, but a way to actually improve the bottom line.

This mix of technologies and capabilities just aren't available to smaller companies, right? That's the theory but the reality is actually quite different.

THE SECRET TO POWERING BUSINESS SUCCESS

Cloud computing – a buzz term widely adopted across the business and tech world – lies at the heart of helping smaller businesses to level the playing field between themselves and the bigger guys.

Its most basic definition is a service that is hosted elsewhere accessed over the internet (see page 11 for further explanation). Perhaps the simplest explanation of cloud computing is to compare it with electricity – this is the most common comparison that is made.

In his authoritative book on computing, *The Big Switch*, US writer Nicholas Carr points out the similarities between computing and the nascent electricity industry in the early part of the 19th century. "As a business resource, information technology today looks a lot like electric power did at the start of the last century [when manufacturers built and maintained their own generators]," he says.

Carr touches on an important point with regard to the way that companies handled electricity. Before the emergence of the National Grid, factories and offices had their own electricity resources. Yet, when the collective supply model came along, these companies were stepping into the unknown. Naturally, there was a reluctance to let go of their own resources and embrace the new way of powering their business.

There's an additional issue though. Companies of old had to spend time looking at their power needs – eating into time, money and valuable human resources – and the same is true of modern-day businesses when it comes to running vast IT departments. They source their own equipment – servers, PCs, storage drives, routers, switches and so on - and hook them together.

They employ techies to make them work, they employ developers to write software and CIOs to manage all these processes. And, unless the company is a hardware company, all of these activities are a sideline to the main business.

ALL CHANGE
There's been a change in business practices in the last 30 or 40 years as organisations have become more streamlined. In the 70s and 80s, most large organisations had their own canteens where cooking and serving staff would supply meals. These were completely irrelevant to the main concern of the business and were gradually eased out – as have

> **Perhaps, the simplest explanation of cloud computing is to compare it with electricity.**

all similar non-essential functions. Yet IT departments remain, costing considerably more than a daily sausage roll and a cup of tea and – seemingly - inviolate.

But just as organisations' own generators disappeared and staff canteens bit the dust, so too has the computer department come under scrutiny. This explains the emergence of cloud computing. It's all about applying the same lessons learned from the electricity industry to modern-day computing.

Carr is not the first to make this parallel. Indeed, the concept of computing as a utility was first suggested by academic Douglas Parkhill in the 1960s.

It should be highlighted that where there are experts, there are opinions. And where opinions exist, they rarely are carbon copies of one another. Indeed, not everyone holds with this idea of cloud as a parallel to electricity.

Cloud technologist James

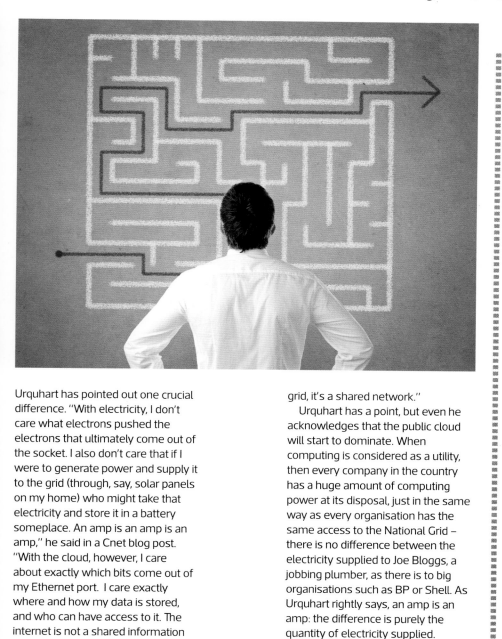

Urquhart has pointed out one crucial difference. "With electricity, I don't care what electrons pushed the electrons that ultimately come out of the socket. I also don't care that if I were to generate power and supply it to the grid (through, say, solar panels on my home) who might take that electricity and store it in a battery someplace. An amp is an amp is an amp," he said in a Cnet blog post. "With the cloud, however, I care about exactly which bits come out of my Ethernet port. I care exactly where and how my data is stored, and who can have access to it. The internet is not a shared information grid, it's a shared network."

Urquhart has a point, but even he acknowledges that the public cloud will start to dominate. When computing is considered as a utility, then every company in the country has a huge amount of computing power at its disposal, just in the same way as every organisation has the same access to the National Grid – there is no difference between the electricity supplied to Joe Bloggs, a jobbing plumber, as there is to big organisations such as BP or Shell. As Urquhart rightly says, an amp is an amp: the difference is purely the quantity of electricity supplied.

There's been a change in business practices over the last 30 or 40 years as organisations become more streamlined.

Computing power is somewhat different. A small business doesn't need to spend a massive amount to keep computer systems running. But companies tend to spend an awful lot of money on IT. If you're a small business, even a PC can represent a substantial part of your budget. And that's before you start adding ever-larger sums for the supporting software. Even essentials such as Microsoft Office cost around £100 for a single user, so the cost of specialist business software could see costs rocketing skywards.

CLOUD AND YOUR BUSINESS

There are several facets to cloud. Companies can use cloud for its hosting (for example, running its company website), for development (if it's the type of small company that employs lots of software coders), for storage (which is an ever-increasing demand on companies' computer spend) and/or for software. Each of these manifestations of cloud has its own nomenclature, pros and cons.

But they all have one thing in common: no business has to buy anything. There's nothing being owned and because, like electricity, users only have to be pay for what's actually been consumed, there's no reason to over-provision and buy more power than is actually needed: no-one likes wasting money.

This leads to one other crucial aspect of cloud computing: no company needs to dip into its capital expenditure budget - everything is part of an operational expense.

It could be argued, though, an expense is an expense whether it's an operational or a capital one. While there are many advantages of moving to a cloud service there are also many questions to ask. We'll go into more detail about some of these in later chapters.

In a nutshell, the definition of cloud (see box out) covers all the key elements of cloud from a customer's point of view:

What is cloud?

It's the buzzword on everybody's lips but what does cloud computing actually mean? It's not been an easy term to define and there have been many different attempts to explain what the term means. Companies have been prone, like Alice's Humpty Dumpty, to define it in a way that suits their own needs.

In some ways it's strange that the term has been so slippery. Millions of us are happy to use such cloud-based services as Facebook, Gmail, Twitter and think nothing of it, yet pinning down an exact definition has been as elusive as grabbing a cloud itself.

In an attempt to stop to the vagaries, the US National Institute of Standards and Technology (NIST) put forward a definition that has now become widely accepted as the closest that the industry has to a definitive answer.

The NIST definition: Cloud computing is a model for enabling ubiquitous, convenient, on-demand network access to a shared pool of configurable computing resources (e.g. networks, servers, storage, applications, and services) that can be rapidly provisioned and released with minimal management effort or service provider interaction. This cloud model promotes availability and is composed of five essential characteristics, three service models, and four deployment models.

- **Self-provisioning so customers can provision facilities without any human interaction;**
- **Delivery of services over a network;**
- **The ability to be accessed by a variety of devices: PCs, netbooks, tablets and smartphones;**
- **Rapid elasticity – the ability to scale up or scale down computing resources and ensure availability.**

From a cloud provider's point of view, a major element of the process is the pooling of computing resources to serve multiple consumers. This is done using a multi-tenant model whereby cloud services are provided to customers as and when they're needed. One of the important factors for cloud service providers is to be able to measure and, even more importantly, to bill accurately.

FEELING SECURE ABOUT THE SECURITY

The factor in cloud services that makes most users nervous is the level of security and within a multi-tenant model this is obviously going to be a major concern. Customers are entrusting some of their sensitive data to a third party and, for example, there is nothing stopping one of that customer's major competitors going to the same cloud provider.

Service providers believe that this concern can be easily dealt with. They've generally had a long history of keeping customers' data safe and have levels of security that far exceed their customers. Take Amazon, one of the leading lights in cloud technology. Millions of us around the world are willing to entrust our personal details and credit cards to the company believing they'll be held safely – why should trusting the company's cloud division, Amazon Web Services, be any different?

In many ways, a more important consideration than security is the location of data. This is for two reasons: the inherent latency within the system, the further away the data is stored, the longer the lag in accessing it.

This is becoming less of a problem as network connections get faster, but it can be a factor to consider.

The second problem is a more serious one, particularly on this side of the Atlantic. There are various EU regulations about where data can be stored. Personal data cannot be held outside the EU, for example. While, within the EU itself, individual countries have stricter guidelines still. This has given some cloud providers large headaches.

Part of the appeal of cloud computing is that unused resources at one data centre can be used by another. If data centres outside the EU cannot be employed to store European customers' data, service providers have to be more careful in marshalling their resources.

Allied to this is a secondary problem: the US Patriot Act. It compels US companies to hand over personal data held on their servers if requested by US authorities. As this applies to European data held on servers located in Europe, this has made some European customers rather nervous.

At the time of publication, the full implications of the Patriot Act are still being worked through.

We've spoken a lot about cloud service providers so far, but another important part of the cloud is the delivery of software – the so-called Software-as-a-Service (SaaS) delivery mechanism. This is a technique that was really pioneered by Salesforce.com with its hosted CRM product, but has since been

> ## The factor in cloud services that makes users most nervous is the level of security.

adopted by countless other cloud-focused companies.

SaaS delivery helps solve various problems within a business – over-provisioning, security updates and licensing among them – and is now widely viewed as the dominant method for providing software.

Cloud computing as a concept has grown quickly and is set to penetrate deeper into the market. According to an oft-cited report from analyst firm Gartner, 20 per cent of enterprises will have no IT departments by the end of 2012. While that plainly didn't happen the impetus is with cloud. It's a technology that's definitely here to stay. ∎

■ CHAPTER 2 LOOKING AT TECHNOLOGY

Talking tech – which product is right for you?

There are many services, technologies and tools competing for attention. We detail some of the key players' offerings so you can decide what is right for you.

WHEN LOOKING AT CLOUD-BASED software, there are many decisions to be made. Cost is obviously a big part of the equation, but it isn't the only thing to bear in mind. It's important to look at how the software integrates with any existing applications you have. You also need to bear in mind

ease of use and ease of maintenance. Can you fix problems yourself when something goes wrong? If not, what's the support like? Does it scale to meet your needs?

There's also the range of options to consider. When equipping your office, you're going to be looking at different

types of software. First up, there's productivity software. In enterprise environments, this is nearly always Microsoft Office, but there are other options in the cloud world. That said, the main choice is going to be between Office 365 – the cloud version of Microsoft's software – and Google Apps.

Then there's the accounting software that you're going to need. There are several choices here:

ranging from cloud-only offerings such as Kashflow to cloud versions from long-established players like Sage. Each of them has advantages and disadvantages – we'll look at both later in this chapter.

It's not just the need for financial applications: there are also the possibilities for storage. Most of the big players have something to offer here: Apple, Google and Microsoft. But there are also two relatively new kids on the block too, in the form of Box and Dropbox. Some might say the latter is a company that almost created the cloud-based storage market by itself.

> **Cost is obviously a big part of the equation but it isn't the only thing to bear in mind.**

DELVING A LITTLE DEEPER
Let's start by looking at productivity software. This has traditionally meant

Office and Exchange mail within most businesses. But the emergence of cloud has meant there's some choice here: Microsoft has developed Office 365 for those companies that want a cloud-based version of traditional Microsoft products. But there's also growing interest in Google Apps, which offers a similar range of services to the Microsoft offering.

They're not quite equal though. Microsoft has a large installed base and a relatively easy migration path from on-premise products to Office 365, while Google Apps does well in green field sites but does get a little bit trickier when migrating from existing Microsoft apps.

PRODUCTIVITY SOFTWARE: OFFICE 365 VERSUS GOOGLE APPS

Office 365 offers cloud-based versions of desktop apps – Exchange mail server with Forefront malware and spam protection, SharePoint document management and Lync Online for communications (presence, instant messaging and audio and video calls). You also get online versions of Word, Excel, PowerPoint, OneNote and Outlook. Some subscriptions even include the full Office Professional Plus suite. There's also an Office 365 marketplace for third-party tools that

work with the service.

Google Apps for Business includes Gmail with Postini spam and malware filtering and basic smartphone management, Calendar and Contacts, Google Docs (including spreadsheets and presentations), Chat, Groups mailing lists and Sites.

You can use the control panel to manage users and what they can do with the Google Apps tools as well as their access to various other Google services like Picasa (which may get more important as Google combines personal and Google Apps accounts into a single account type) and add third-party services from the Google Apps Marketplace.

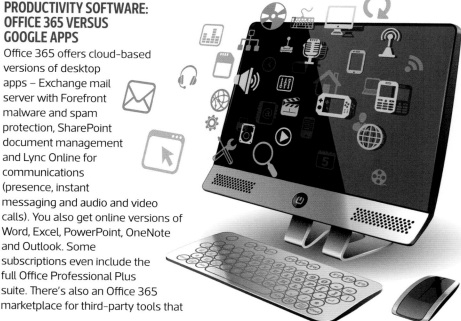

ADMIN CONSOLE

The Office 365 admin console provides a pane for switching between managing users, services and domains (clear explanations of what the main management tools are for are next to the links to manage them). There are also handy shortcuts at the bottom of the window containing links to relevant resources and community discussions.

Google Apps has two levels of administration rights; the 'super admin' who has full access and admins to whom you can delegate some administration tasks. You can also give different users a mix of rights but you have to remember who can do what.

Microsoft takes a different approach. A key part of the way that Office 365 is configured is through the use of Roles.

Microsoft has provided five named admin roles as well as a user role. On top of this, there is the option for a Partner Delegated Administrator, which is for organisations that use a third party to manage Office 365.

SETTING UP THE SERVICE

There's a setup guide to get you started on Google Apps which walks you through things like verifying the domain you're using, creating user accounts and changing your records to point to Gmail (you need your own domain to use Google Apps). It's mostly clear and simple, but the duplicated instructions and

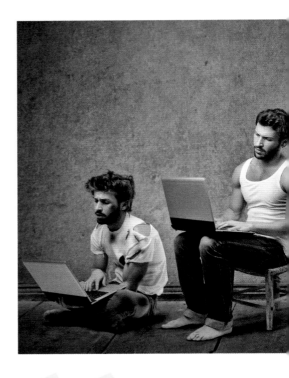

You also need to bear in mind ease of use and ease of maintenance.

sometimes circuitous interface make setup a very fragmented experience. Indeed, the Postini integration is particularly tricky.

Security for Office 365 is handled by a system called Forefront Online Protection for Exchange (FOPE) which also takes a bit of configuration, particularly when it comes to spam.

You can create Office 365 users

You can set up Google Apps users one by one in the control panel. To migrate Exchange mailboxes, there are two options: Google Apps Migration for Microsoft Exchange, which requires no programming ability (but can't be used for old – pre-2003 – versions of Exchange) or the Google Apps Email Migration API, which supports every version of Exchange but does require some technical know-how.

MAIL ADMIN OPTIONS

Office 365 has a simple interface for basic admin options like managing passwords and security groups but you can also use the full Exchange Online interface. This is identical to the web interface for Exchange Server, so it will be very familiar to Exchange admins. You get a set of tools for setting up features like role-based access control, transport rules (such as adding disclaimers to external email) and reports to help track down any problems along with auditing logs for compliance. If you don't need them you can stick to the basics and be up and running within minutes.

individually – assigning admin rights and turning on services for them at the same time. Importantly, you can also connect to an existing on-premise Exchange server and migrate users and mailboxes, or synchronise with your Active Directory to manage Office 365 users with roles and policies in the same way you manage existing users (so you can delete a user in AD and they're removed from Exchange Online). You even get PowerShell cmdlets (a neat bit of jargon coined by Microsoft that's used by techies to describe an automated script used in its PowerShell language) that let you configure Office 365 from the command line.

With Gmail, you don't get to control the mail server, although you do have control over routing and mail gateway settings. The options are mostly on the level of setting up a URL for users, or allowing Docs results to show up in a Gmail search. This doesn't matter too much. The big advantage of using Google Apps as far as most small businesses are (continued on P22...)

Q&A Karen Ainley, product manager, Sage

We spoke to Sage's Karen Ainley about the tech challenges SMBs face and the growing importance of cloud when it comes to accountancy.

1 How important is cloud computing and Software-as-a-Service (SaaS) going to be to small businesses in future?

There is a move towards cloud-based offerings and subscription pricing. Cloud computing and the increasing trend in mobile working is already prominent in the CRM and HCM market place and becoming a growing trend in the Accounting and ERP market place.

Growing customer experience of online consumer applications creates an expectation of real-time data access anywhere, anytime. This consumer experience is changing customer demands in their working life, particularly in the technology and software market. In a cloud adoption survey conducted by Microsoft it was found that 39 per cent of SMBs expect to be paying for one or more cloud services within three years. SaaS products are believed to already have about a 20 per cent share in the micro and small business accounting space.

> The move to cloud/ Saas-based systems is one of the biggest changes the software industry has ever faced.

2 What are the main issues facing small businesses moving to this type of software delivery?

The move to cloud/SaaS-based systems is one of the biggest changes the software industry has ever faced and concerns will arise as business owners get to grips with the idea of having their systems and data held off site.

In highly regulated industries – who would generally prefer to manage data in-house – the decision is even harder to make as concerns over security arise. Finding a provider they can trust to handle this for them is critical.

When sourcing a provider the customer should ensure they select a brand they trust as well as seeking vendors that utilise data centres that comply with key industry standards, such as ISO/IEC 27001:2005, for security and reliability.

Integrating other applications a customer may use with their new cloud-based software will also be a concern as they explore how to ensure their business can

trade as normal in this new world. Looking at the project from a wider perspective and taking into account software used in other areas when planning will help with the company's road map to cloud enablement.

3 What are the main IT challenges an SMB has to overcome?

Typically, firms want to be able to focus on their core business without distraction. IT overheads, such as servers, infrastructure and IT personnel are major costs and cloud eliminates the need for such expense. Businesses want as little disruption as possible when implementing new systems, and cloud systems with one-click deployment drastically reduce the pain and ensure a business is up and running quickly.

Data back-ups often prove troublesome for small businesses with a large percentage failing. This can prove catastrophic when trying to restore this back-up and the business realises that their data is lost. Data back-ups and recovery come as standard with cloud systems meaning businesses need not worry about the validity of the backup or the time and cost it takes to ensure that this business-critical function takes place.

4 Why should an SMB use Sage rather than something from cloud–only players?

Sage has more than 30 years' experience in software development and supporting SMBs. We aim to give customers more choice in how they deploy and pay for their software. We know that not all customers are the same and we aim to meet the needs of everyone. Our products are future-proofed and built on modern, robust technology platforms. This ensures, that, as you grow, we can grow with you and flex to meet your needs. More than 23,000 of the UK's largest businesses, including more than one third of the FTSE 100, choose Sage software to support their business and there are more than six million Sage customers worldwide.

We are working closely with Microsoft on its Windows Azure platform to bring our flagship SMB product Sage 200 to market. Two industry giants working together gives you a slicker solution built on industry-leading technology and confidence the future of your business is in safe hands.

5 How will the cloud version of Sage 200 integrate with other software?

Sage 200 integrates with both Microsoft Office 365 and Microsoft office on-premise, ensuring customers can integrate with Microsoft Office regardless of deployment method. Customers are supported on modern and up-to-date technology platforms. Through our 900-strong developer network we offer integration with many third-party software products and services.

■ For more information visit **www.sage.co.uk**

concer... is that there is less faffing around too - though administering email accounts can be tricky. With Google looking after the mail server, most businesses will find they don't need more admin options.

There's little difference between the two options when it comes to mailbox limits. Indeed, both Google Apps and Office 365 have a, fairly generous, mailbox limit of 25GB. There's isn't an archiving option from Gmail, but with Office 365 you have a choice between third-party archiving services or a specific Office 365 plan with unlimited storage when it comes to email archiving.

> One of the growing demands within any workplace is the need for chat or messaging services.

MOBILE SUPPORT

As you'd expect, Google Apps for Business works especially well with Android devices.

You can set a policy that enforces a password of a particular strength, wipe lost devices and remotely locate or lock a phone. Google Apps also operates a full range of services on iPhone. All Google business apps are available from the iTunes store.

There's also a connector to allow you to manage BlackBerry users of Google Apps from a BlackBerry Enterprise Server, and options for applying password and other device policies to smartphones using Google Sync or Exchange ActiveSync. But, as might be expected, the company offers no support for Microsoft Windows phones. But Microsoft customers are not wholly ignored. In spring

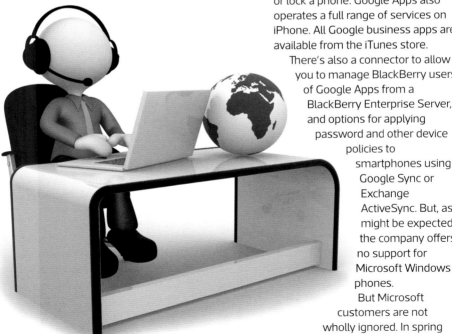

2013, Google rolled out services from QuickOffice – it acquired the company in 2012 – that allows customers to view, create and edit Word, Excel and PowerPoint documents on iPhones and Android devices. Google had already launched a version for iPads.

While Google offers easy ways to access other software on mobiles, device security is not quite so straightforward as this requires an app to be downloaded from the Android Marketplace. Turning on device security stops them using Android Marketplace until the application is installed.

Office 365 offers a complete range of services. Exchange Online gives you the same mobile device management as Exchange Server using ActiveSync Policies which work on all smartphones including Android, iPhone, BlackBerry and Symbian as well as Windows phones.

There's enhanced security: you can enforce strong passwords and encryption, control individual device features (like Bluetooth), configure sync options like whether attachments can be downloaded on a phone and wipe devices automatically if the password is entered incorrectly too many times. You can also block or quarantine specific mobile devices.

MESSAGING

One of the growing demands within any workplace is the need for chat or messaging services. Users like seeing who is available when a quick response is needed. It's a feature that may be more appreciated within enterprises but it could well be an option for small businesses too.

Both Google and Microsoft offer such features within their productivity suites. Google Chat is the same simple tool available to the public; users can see presence statuses for Google Apps contacts inside Gmail and start a text, voice or video chat from there. Alternatively they can use the Windows Google Talk software for text and voice chat or file transfer. Management is minimal; you can

block chat outside the organisation or just warn users but you aren't able to block file transfers.

Microsoft's Lync Online lets you choose whether users can transfer files, make audio or video calls and talk to people outside the business or just colleagues. Users can see each other's presence and status in Outlook and Outlook Web Access (including information from someone's Exchange calendar), and in any Office app where you're collaborating. It's possible to start a chat, voice or video call from there or from the Lync client.

However, there's going to be a transformation of chat (and voice) capability in the summer of 2013 when Microsoft begins work on the integration of Skype (the voice over IP service) with Lync. The company has announced that Lync-Skype connectivity for IM and voice will be available to customers by the end of June. Microsoft says this will herald an

Users like seeing who is available when a quick response is needed.

era of what it calls B2X capability, where the boundaries between the business market and the consumer one become blurred – from the bedroom to the boardroom is the phrase coined by the Microsoft marketing department.

When it comes to messaging, both products offer the basic resources but the forthcoming changes to Microsoft Lync should mean that it's going to prove more appealing to more sophisticated businesses.

SUPPORT

Google Apps also offers 24/7 phone support. That said, this service is only for critical problems that involve more than half your users and affect the Google Apps Web services. If the problem is with mobile emails you'd be stuck with email support, which doesn't cover weekends.

Google Apps has a flat price of £33 per user per year for the basic service (it's also charged at £3.30 per user per month). There is another option: Google Apps for Business with Vault costs £6.60 per month but offers a range of archiving and retrieval services.

Office 365 has a more granular pricing plan, with a range of prices. The starting price is for Office 365 Home Premium –which licenses up to five devices - for £79.99 per year or £7.99 per month.

This price includes 20GB of SkyDrive cloud storage and 60 minutes of Skype calls per month (Microsoft bought the VoIP service in 2012).

Most small businesses would be interested in the P1 Office 365 plan. This provides businesses between one and 50 employees with Office Web Apps, Exchange Online, SharePoint Online, Lync Online and an external website. It is priced at £4 per user per month.

CONCLUSION

There's little doubt that of the two productivity suites Office 365 is the more mature product. Microsoft has a

Choosing an IaaS provider

It's not just about choosing software services. You could be looking for a company to host your servers too.

It's a market that's dominated by Amazon Web Services (AWS) but there have been plenty of other companies offering virtual servers or machines (VMs) and associated storage resources hosted within the provider's data centre, usually on shared physical servers.

SMBs will access those VMs to run specific applications via a self-service web portal that allows the user to set up an account, specifying the compute and storage resources they need – whether that's on a pay-as-you-go basis or by reserved instances.

Many small businesses will select an IaaS provider by choosing the cheapest service. Unfortunately, it's often hard to ascertain which provider's service is cheapest. For example, customers may want to upload their own workloads but this could be expensive and they prefer to use standard, pre-defined VM images from the cloud service provider's library. These are offered loaded with specific applications and operating systems, often with different complements of CPU cores, RAM and hard disk capacity. These are sized differently and often use different manufacturers' CPUs and clockspeeds, all of which can affect performance, making it hard to assess cost.

On top of that, there's the added difficulty of network availability – all cloud services require a resilient broadband connection and this could vary in price. There's also the question of service level agreements – what sort of service are you interested in? Do you want additional resilience? What about security? There are

long history in business software and it shows in the way that Office 365 has been developed.

Google doesn't have that history and Google Apps is a relatively new product. Having said that, there are obviously some serious users of the software out there and the company is not standing still: Google is regularly updating Google Apps.

Because the company doesn't have the long history in productivity software Microsoft can boast,

Google's patches and upgrades arrive at irregular intervals. This shouldn't matter too much though: one of the big advantages of cloud services is the continuous and regular improvements. And maintaining on-premise software is a far more daunting proposition.

If you opt for Microsoft, on the other hand, you will get a range of updates at regular intervals. You may prefer this for planning purposes, or you may be perfectly happy with Google's

different levels of data security available – not every business wants every single byte of data totally locked down.

Regulated firms may have other demands: geographical location of data centres and detailed audit trails, for example.

The final piece of the jigsaw is support. Do you want 24/7 phone contact? Are you happy with email support? Most businesses without a dedicated IT department aren't.

There are so many variables, it's almost impossible to give definitive guidelines as to what IaaS offering an SMB should use.

AWS is the clear leader, but Google, Microsoft and Rackspace - and a multitude of smaller UK service providers (Claranet, FastHosts, Memset and UKFast among many others) - offer SMB access to the cloud.

It's a question of talking to them and finding out which one best suits your needs.

Talk to several providers, talk to their customers and get a feel of which one you're happiest with – as with software providers, there's no right or wrong answer.

approach; different individuals take different stances on this. It's what you're happy with that counts.

The two services are both powerful but they suit different audiences. If your business already uses Microsoft tools, Office 365 is the logical progression, giving you server workloads that integrate with and make the most of your existing investments. You could still choose to implement Google Apps but you know that your workload is going to

be much tougher.

It's especially useful if you're looking to run a mix of on-premise and cloud services, having to manage both Active Directory and the Google Apps control panel is a lot more work than if you're running everything through Microsoft software.

On the other hand, if you are setting up from scratch and have no systems at all then Google Apps is the easier option. Google has a reputation for simplicity – everyone can use Gmail

after all – and this translates into Google Apps. It's closer to a true cloud service, in that much of the management is handled by Google itself. It's certainly more limited in scope than Office 365 but, in its most basic form, it's cheaper and may do exactly what you want. Certainly, if your business uses Android mobiles and tablets, you may find it the more appropriate option.

There's no right or wrong answer. It comes down to personal taste and your existing systems: both products are strong and have a lot to offer the emerging business. If you're looking to work without a recognised IT department, one of the two is going to be absolutely essential for the future development of your business.

OTHER SOFTWARE

Productivity software is just one part of the equation. Companies looking to use cloud services have to consider a range of software options.

One big requirement is storage as there's an ever-increasing need to retain data, due to the increasing computerisation of records, the growth of larger (multimedia) files and, in some regulated environments, more stringent compliance demands.

> The two services are both powerful but they suit different audiences.

Dropbox is arguably the archetypal cloud storage service and has become almost the default system for home users. But it's made its way into businesses too and has become a popular tool. Because it's so user-friendly, it's handy for keeping key files up to date and accessible across desktop and laptop PCs and mobile devices.

But it's not the only option. Microsoft has been keen to offer its SkyDrive product as an alternative, while Box offers support for businesses and Google Drive offers integration with Google Apps.

We'll now look at all four options, considering their ease of use, features offered and performance speed. There is some variation here so businesses can choose which one suits them best.

> **There's no right or wrong answer. It comes down to personal taste and your existing systems.**

BOX

The Box for Business plan offers companies 1TB of storage space that can be shared between three and 500 users and the Box Sync applet enables synchronisation between a My Box Files folder across multiple user machines.

The Business plan comes with a comprehensive admin panel that allows you to add and remove users, assign rights to specific folders and monitor file uploads, downloads and changes. Files and folders can be shared with other Box users by inviting them to collaborate, or with non-Box users via an email link. Once you have collaborators, it's easy for everyone to comment on files and assign tasks and deadlines to their colleagues. In a way, Box is becoming less a cloud storage service and more a cloud-based workflow tool.

Other useful features include versioning (the ability to lock files against further versions) and mobile apps for Android, BlackBerry, iOS and Windows Phone. What's more, plug-in apps mean Box can integrate with Microsoft Office or Google Apps, so you can save files to and from Box from within the relevant Office suites.

With the Business plan, Box is a strong cloud storage service. The web-based interface is easy to use and there are plenty of security options, including SSL encrypted transfers, and – unlike some rival services –files are encrypted while at rest. Speeds are also good with some pretty sharp upload times.

The biggest issue is the price. Box for Business costs £11.99 per user per month, which is expensive in comparison to the Dropbox, Google and Microsoft options. The file preview features also don't work

> ## There is some variation here so businesses can choose which one suits them best.

quite as well as Google or Microsoft's.

Box is well worth considering for its advanced administration and collaboration features, but it's not as quick and intuitive as Dropbox or as effectively tied into Windows and Office as SkyDrive – nor as affordable.

DROPBOX

Dropbox for Teams, the business version of the popular service, was launched in 2012. It now scales up for Business use too. Plans start at $795 per year for five users with a pooled 1TB of space, and scales up at $125 per additional user, with each one bringing in an extra 200GB of capacity. Usage can be monitored and managed from a central console.

The service offers an easy-to-setup client on every machine, with a special 'Dropbox' folder placed on each hard drive. Files saved or dropped in the Dropbox are automatically synchronised across all systems connected to that account.

Dropbox's key advantage is the ease and efficiency of sharing. Files and folders can be shared with other Dropbox users through email invitations and, once shared, the files

will synchronise automatically, with notifications when another user adds or changes the file. Files will synchronise across a LAN as well as the internet, helping to keep business bandwidth costs down. Non-Dropbox users can also get file access via a web link.

All these features make Dropbox incredibly useful, and for many smaller businesses the free 2GB option could be enough. You can access files from tablets and phones and even upload photos and videos direct. However, there are limitations. For instance, there are no built-in apps to preview or edit office documents, either, though many mobile apps, including QuickOffice and Documents To Go, will open and save documents direct to and from a Dropbox account. It's also one of the speediest options out there.

One big concern may be security. Files are stored using 256-bit AES encryption and the service uses SSL for data transfer, while the actual data is held on Amazon's S3 servers, with high security and multiple levels of redundancy. However, there have been a number of security issues with the service which caused many users to worry about its viability. In response, Dropbox has improved its security monitoring and introduced two-step authentication in autumn 2012; time will tell whether this is enough to allay fears.

GOOGLE DRIVE

Google Drive combines Google Apps with Dropbox-like functionality.

The interface is the normal one for Google services but it offers companies 5GB of free, general purpose storage space per user, which can be increased to 25GB, 100GB or more through upgrades. A downloadable Google Drive applet creates a Google Drive folder on your PC, and then enables synchronisation of that folder across devices, in the vein of Dropbox.

Whether you like the user interface is a matter of personal taste. There are good points about the stripped-back look and simple presentation, and Google's strong search facilities make it easier to find files in a crowded folder.

However, Google Drive doesn't have as much of the easy one-click functionality of Dropbox or the Windows/Office integration of SkyDrive, and it's frustrating that to, say, share a folder, you have to go to Google Drive in your browser and right-click on the folder sitting there. It can feel slightly clunky.

Google Drive's biggest advantage is its easy integration with Google Apps.

If your company uses Gmail then being able to share files and folders quickly with contacts in your address book, or sending documents as Google Drive links rather than attachments works well. Google Drive has some catching up to do with Dropbox, Box and SkyDrive when it comes to mobile support. As you'd expect, Android is fully supported but support for other devices is not quite so strong.

Google Drive makes most sense as part of Google Apps, where it can play the role of the hub in a document management and collaboration, or in smaller businesses where Gmail and Google Docs are already deployed. Otherwise, Dropbox is more efficient and easier to use, while SkyDrive's seamless office integration can't be dismissed. However, Google Drive is extremely cheap for what you get, so if your focus is on the bottom line, it's a viable choice.

It's quick and easy to preview office documents, PDFs and most common photo and video file formats, whether you have any specific software installed or not.

However, while you can edit Microsoft Office docs from your desktop Google Drive using the standard Microsoft Office applications, doing so within the browser requires importing them in a Google Docs format then exporting the changed version later – not exactly a streamlined process. Google Docs can also struggle to maintain the fidelity of complex documents.

SKYDRIVE

The integration of Microsoft SkyDrive with Office and Windows 8 offers much to small businesses. The product provides 7GB, free, as part of a Windows Live account which can easily be upgraded by 20, 50 or 100GB.

SkyDrive has been revamped for Windows 8, but it works on Windows 7 and Windows Vista. A SkyDrive desktop app gives companies a specific SkyDrive folder which works

in much the same way as Dropbox.

Office files stored on SkyDrive can be edited from within the browser. Customers can also save files straight back out to SkyDrive, and there's no need to mess around with importing and exporting files.

Features for sharing media work pretty well with built-in photo, video and audio playback facilities. Files and folders can be shared with other users by right-clicking on them, selecting 'Share' and emailing a link. It's also easy to post the link to Facebook, LinkedIn or Twitter, or even generate code to embed the file on a web page – although the ease of use may be a security concern.

> **Google Drive is extremely cheap for what you get, so if your focus is on the bottom line, it's a viable choice.**

The main benefit of SkyDrive is that it's heavily tied into both Windows 8 and Office. Windows 8 has its own SkyDrive app as standard, while Office 2013 makes a user's SkyDrive account the default place for saving new documents and it's easy to keep documents synced across multiple PCs and backed up in the cloud.

Security is a concern though. SkyDrive uses SSL to encrypt files during transport, but these files are unencrypted once at rest on Microsoft's servers. Given that Microsoft's servers are themselves heavily secured this might not be a concern, but it leaves SkyDrive behind Box in this respect. SkyDrive is also slightly slower when it comes to uploads than its competitors.

If your business plans to move to Windows 8 and Office 2013, SkyDrive is the product that makes most sense. But even if you're not a user of these products, it provides plenty for SMBs. Box has better features, while Dropbox offers more simplicity, but SkyDrive offers a good compromise.

ACCOUNTING SOFTWARE

While the storage space is competitive with little to choose between the offerings, any firm looking for accounting options

> **Though the ease of use may be a security concern...**

is spoiled for choice. It's another area where there's healthy competition but, in some ways, it's very different from the storage market.

There are several companies with cloud offerings so the business has plenty to choose from – but there are some real differentiators here with each product having a mixture of strengths and weaknesses. You can choose according to your own particular demands.

KashFlow, FreeAgent and Xero all came to market as cloud-based players solving the financial headaches experienced by many small businesses. Then there's the long-established doyen of small business accounting, Sage, which also announced a cloud version of its software.

Accounting practices have been quick to recognise real-time shared access to financial data has a positive impact on their ability to provide better services.

Let's take a look at what they offer...

KASHFLOW

This offers a broad accounting system that appeals to many types of small business user and especially those that only need something relatively simple: you could describe it as 'book-keeping plus.'

The product has many points of automation. For example, it can be set up to automate billing, which is useful for companies who invoice for the same amount each month.

KashFlow also understands the type of inbound invoices that are being received, enabling the service to allocate to the correct general ledger account code. Unusually, KashFlow allows users to create custom fields for billing and offers billing in any currency.

In terms of APIs, KashFlow has a large set of integrations and add-ons. The list is extensive including payroll and payment processors - key requirements for any business. KashFlow offers simple pricing at £17.99 a month.

FREEAGENT

FreeAgent was established as a response to a common problem: the need to submit spreadsheets to the accountant for later production.

It's a rather specialised product aimed at the freelance services market although a partnership with Barclays MWB has seen it expand.

The main problem the founders saw was that freelancers almost never know what their tax position

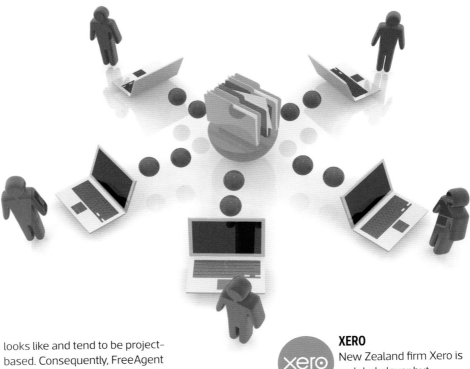

looks like and tend to be project-based. Consequently, FreeAgent delivers a tax estimate rather than a definitive value and project estimates can be turned into invoices, including rechargeable out-of-pocket expenses. FreeAgent is also being engineered to automate as much of the routine accounts processing tasks as possible. In March 2013, the company introduced a new payroll system that enables easier filing of tax returns to HMRC.

Perhaps where FreeAgent slips behind other competing services is in the lack of a true multi-currency option - despite this being promised to users some time ago. Pricing is tiered and starts at £15 a month, rising to £25 for UK companies.

XERO

New Zealand firm Xero is a global player but doesn't have the same presence in the UK. Like KashFlow, Xero started with the idea that accounting should be easy. Its appeal is to businesses that want more than KashFlow offers but do not want to be on a more vertical market solution like FreeAgent.

Xero built-in automated bank feeds from the start and today has feeds from more than 5,000 global financial institutions. Its history as an overseas player means that it's particularly strong when it comes to handling multi-currency.

Where Xero has outshone the competition is in mobile offerings called Touch. It's particularly strong on iPhone, although the company has now developed an Android version. Like the other products, Xero pricing is tiered and starts from £12 a month.

SAGE

Although Sage dominates the desktop-based enterprise accounting space in the UK, it has been late to the cloud. However, Sage's entry to this crowded market adds credibility to cloud-based accounting services and its own offering, One Accounts, offers plenty to the small business.

Aimed at sole traders or very small businesses, it doesn't assume any financial knowledge but an Accountant edition gives your accountant remote access to your version of the software.

One Accounts' overview summary charts a business' bank balance, alongside current year sales and expenses and nominal profit and the five most recent unpaid invoices. It supports both service and product-based businesses and, handily, lets you store details of both types to save time when completing invoices. However, it doesn't offer the option to scan and upload receipts. That said, it does offer a straightforward VAT return feature.

On the downside, One Accounts' banking features are comparatively weak. Unlike FreeAgent, there's no direct bank integration, nor is there manual reconciliation feature as effective as Xero's. Reporting choices

> ## Sage's entry to this crowded market adds credibility to cloud-based accounting services.

are sparse: there are only five reports available, compared to the dozens available in KashFlow: although the main ones are included. The basic version is lacking some functions, such as creating journal entries or customising the chart of accounts. These are only available in the Accountant edition. While reports can be exported to Excel, you can't import data, other than contacts and product or service details, from other apps.

In short, it's a rudimentary, one-user service priced at £12 per month. This includes 24-hour support.

Most small businesses will want to concentrate on the areas mentioned so far: the productivity suite; storage services and accounting. However, there are several other areas where companies may see some benefit.

> ## The cloud version of Sage 200 is a way for Sage to shake-up the way it offers its software.

THE BEST OF THE REST

The most obvious of these is customer relationship management (CRM), an area where the clear market leader is Salesforce.com. This is a product that has been designed to be easy to use as much of the impetus for its adoption has come from sales departments.

However, it's not the easiest product to integrate with other systems, nor is it the cheapest out there – many small businesses may find it easier to simply turn to something else.

One option that may be appealing is SugarCRM. Non-technical business owners may find it easier to set up as well as benefiting from the technical support. Its roots in open source mean that users can also change SugarCRM to fit in with their own business requirements.

Businesses may also want to consider enterprise resource planning (ERP). As the name suggests, this is software aimed at the larger business. It offers integration of a variety of software functions: accounting, CRM, stock control, sales and so on into one single product, improving the way that business is reported. It's overkill for most small businesses but increasingly companies are seeing some benefits in using ERP.

The enterprise market is dominated by two players: SAP and Oracle, although Microsoft has a presence here too – these companies offer ERP products that are far too complex for the small business. But when it comes to smaller players, it's worth looking at NetSuite and Sage. NetSuite has a long-standing cloud presence and has been one of the trailblazers in this area. But it is expensive for small businesses and could be overkill.

Sage is set to release a new ERP system, Sage 200, aimed squarely at the small business market. However, it won't be available until June 2013 so it's too early to get a feel for what's being

offered although there have been some early trial users

SAGE FOR THE CLOUD ERA

The cloud version of Sage 200 is a way for Sage to shake up the way it offers its software. The company developed the product in autumn 2012 and has been offering it to various beta customers to ascertain how it will be received and to iron out any potential problems before the launch this summer.

One of the trialists was Donna Rae, accounting manager for Electraction, a manufacturer of batteries for forklift trucks, and a long-standing Sage customer. "We've been a Sage 100

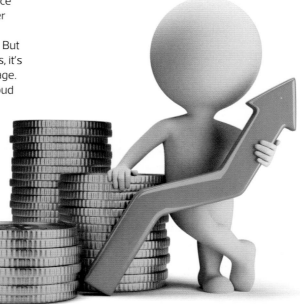

> The cloud part is very beneficial for us. I can enter data when I'm away from the office and it's automatically updated.

the server went down but was convinced by Sage's reassurances on the amount of backup.

As far as Rae is concerned, the huge advantage for Electraction is that she no longer has to be in the office to access her accounts.

"The cloud part is very beneficial for us," she says. "I can enter data when I'm away from the office – and it's automatically updated."

She says the move to cloud has been a smooth one, with only a few minor hiccups, mainly due to the way that data is presented in a slightly different way from the way it was handled in Sage 100.

Since the implementation of Sage 200 within Electraction, the process has been greatly simplified by the launch of a new portal from Sage. This will enable much faster

user and obviously had to upgrade it," says Rae.

Moving from on-premise technology to cloud was obviously a radical departure for Electraction and one that was a new experience for Rae.

"I was aware of cloud," says Rae, who admitted she had a few concerns about security but was mollified by the thought that Sage was a reputable company. She was worried about what would happen if

installation and an easier way of performing backups – it's a process that eases things for customers.

TIME TO DECIDE...

It's impossible to give more than a flavour of the range of products out there. There are literally hundreds of apps that offer something to small businesses. They range in price, in functionality, in usability and integration capabilities. This book can only give a glimpse of the possibilities out there.

Anyone wanting to know more can keep an eye on www.cloudpro.co.uk, which regularly reports on cloud services for small business.

Another useful resource for any companies looking to assess small business apps is GetApp.com. It provides a list of all of the major (and some not so major) business apps, with full details of their functionality and some independent assessments.

Many of the companies mentioned here offer free trials of their software so you can get a chance to play with the apps to see if they suit your business.

Talk to your colleagues, your friends and associates to see what software they use – there's no such thing as the right software for every single business.

What may be right for you, may not be right for the business down the road and vice versa.

One thing is very clear though, the opportunity for small businesses to add real IT functionality to their processes has never been greater.

If you've ever cast envious eyes at the power of large enterprise systems, now is the time to really start to play catch up. ■

sion of
liability
ment, w
Compliance
Responsibility
Illegal
Legal

■ CHAPTER 3 LEGAL ISSUES

The letter of the law

After the basics and the deeper dive into the technology, even the smallest of businesses have to comply with the laws of the land and their industries...

SO, YOU'VE MADE THE decision to move to implement an IT system based around cloud computing. You've decided what software you need, you've sourced the vendors and now you're ready to move with a service provider. The next question is, how to draw up a contract to ensure that you're protected.

One of the problems with this is that service providers' contracts tend to be very much loaded in favour of the suppliers. Indeed, they hold the whip hand. That said, there are still areas to be negotiated and it's not quite as restrictive you might first think. The important thing, as with most activities in business or life, is to prepare thoroughly.

There are three main areas to concentrate on: reliability, security and liability. All potential customers should be paying attention to what a cloud providers' policy in these three areas is.

Compliance

RELIABILITY

Reliability covers a multitude of sins all referring to technical performance of a cloud provider's service. Do the company's servers break down? What mirroring options does the firm have in place? What monitoring systems are in use?

Customers should be prepared to carry out due diligence on cloud providers and assess their performance. Look at the company's past performance – does it have a good reputation?

What's important to realise, however, is concerns over reliability shouldn't blind you to thinking that everything would be perfect if it were hosted in-house.

Running your own systems will

> There are three main areas to concentrate on: reliability, security and liability.

take a great deal of time, require specialist expertise and constant maintenance. So even if not everything is 100 per cent perfect, there's no guarantee that what they'll be offering is something worse than you can do yourself.

Cloud providers will say that managing data centres is their core business. Many will also claim that they're much more reliable at managing this infrastructure than end-user organisations will be. However, while it's true that cloud providers tend to have more robust and better-managed infrastructures, the customer needs more reassurance than that. It's vital that all the fine details are built-in to the service. And the type of cloud provider is important here. Indeed, one factor to bear in mind is that buying a standard package from a larger operator will leave very little room to manoeuvre, while – at the other end of the scale - customising an offering from a smaller reseller could provide you with a much more tailored experience.

SECURITY

When it comes to security, there are a couple of factors to consider. Financial companies will have the demands of the Financial Services Act to conform with and all companies will have to consider the Data Protection Act and the scrutiny of the Information Commissioner. Those who don't pay attention to the rules and regulations are heading for much more than a slapped wrist – offending organisations can be hit by big fines. For example, in 2009, the FSA fined HSBC £3 million for losing data.

Just because you're an SMB, don't be too cavalier about data protection. In fact, you need to be more aware because, unlike large enterprises, you most likely won't have a security or data protection specialist on-hand to keep you out of trouble.

Let's be blunt about this: the liability for any privacy or security breaches lies with the cloud customer. That's you. Therefore, you have to be very circumspect about handing over information to a third party, ie the cloud provider.

It's very important for companies to ensure that cloud providers are taking proper steps to protect data. Are they keeping it inside the EU where there is adequate protection for data, rather than sending it over to the US or further afield? If the provider can't guarantee where the data will be stored, walk away. One thing though, there's no legal necessity to host inside the UK – just as long as it's being hosted in the EU. It does offer greater peace of mind, however, if the data centre is at the other end of the motorway rather than the other side of Europe.

Although the customer is ultimately liable, there are steps that can be taken to mitigate risks. The contract should include where the data is held and to whom it can be released. There should be an indemnity clause meaning that the cloud provider takes all possible precautions to avoid breaches as well as taking legal responsibility for any losses. These precautions should be set out in writing and the level of legal responsibility should also be defined.

Compensation is one thing, the ultimate sanction, however, is that market forces will come into play. If a company loses data, then its reputation will suffer – cloud companies are going to stand or fall by their reliability and a few security

Responsibility

A duty or obligation upon one ... moral, or legal accountability in to behave correctly in respect o ability or authority to act or de take decisions independently.

breaches will quickly destroy that.

LIABILITY

This is if the worst happens and something goes very wrong.

Again, levels of compensation need to be placed in the contract, but be wary of this area. A big pot of money will be of little use to a company that has gone bust.

Some cloud providers try to exclude liability, in a similar way to the approach insurance companies take when deciding not to pay out on their policies. The customer could get around this problem by taking out an insurance product of their own, though. As the cloud market becomes more mature, we will probably see insurance companies offer precisely these sort of policies, so it's worth looking – and shopping – around.

There is another option. Some cloud providers will offer protection but this will involve paying a higher fee for a Gold or Platinum type service. This approach could mean that the cloud company will be offering a more robust service, based on a high quality data centre, with better monitoring facilities, perhaps with a backup data centre for added resilience. Or it could be based on the fact the cloud company is prepared to pay more if things go wrong, in which case see our previous comments about money being of little use to a company that no longer exists.

RESELLERS

There is one further point to consider. All discussion so far has been about a contract between a single customer and a single supplier. But this won't always be the case. Indeed, many cloud providers buy services from another cloud provider (in fact, some could buy via a broker and use cloud services from several providers).

This kind of 'white labelling' introduces new complications. The customer will be signing on the reseller's terms but there could well be a clash with the cloud hosting company. For example, the cloud company could be providing a bronze level service while the reseller could be offering a gold one. That's a bit of a disconnect. Or, you could have a contract with one provider guaranteeing data is held in Europe but it then buys cloud capacity from another supplier based in the US.

There is one way of getting round this. When you sign a contract, make sure it explicitly states whether your supplier will be buying capacity from another. If it does, then ensure there's a pass-through clause – this is where the reseller supplies services from a named supplier such as Amazon or Microsoft.

There is going to be a lot of activity in the cloud space in the next few years. And there's going to be a degree of consolidation too. One thing that will help separate the wheat from the chaff when it comes to service providers is

Some cloud providers try to exclude liability...

to check their accreditation. The Cloud Industry Forum (CIF) offers a form of certification (although companies self-certify themselves, so it's not wholly rigorous) as does the international standards organisation (ISO). But there's no substitute for your own due diligence.

We've provided tales about the three big areas to look at – reliability, security and liability – let's now look at some other factors in the perfect contract.

ACCEPTANCE

We've mentioned service acceptance already, but what does it actually mean? This is a hugely crucial question that must be answered extremely clearly in the contract for your service. The moment you accept a service is generally synonymous with when you start paying for it. Many vendors will try to define the "acceptance" of service as depending entirely upon them saying it's ready for you to use, based either on some internal criterion or its conformance with some stipulated standard. Needless to say, you shouldn't take this as the whole story. Imagine you're signing up with a cloud service provider and part of

Server provider contracts

There are three types of clause in a service provider contract:

- Clauses that are relevant to the service you're using: ensure you agree with them, and shout if you don't, because you're going to be bound by them.

- Clauses that are relevant to services that you're not using: either insist on them being struck out, or if that's not acceptable to the supplier then insist on the master service agreement explicitly stating that those clauses don't apply.

- Clauses that are relevant to service that you're using, but which the provider says: "Yes, that's just there because the lawyers insisted, we'd never actually use it": be very afraid, and insist they're struck out or noted as irrelevant.

In the last case, if the provider won't strike the clauses out, point out that since they just told you they'd never use them, their refusal to strike them out implies that they're either stupid or lying. It's, unfortunately, very often the latter.

the deal is that they'll be installing some network links between your sites and theirs (it's a common thing to do – not all cloud services need to be delivered over the public internet, after all).

By default there's every chance that they will deem the links "acceptable" when they have been shown to be error-free and to route the various subnets you're using correctly. You should, however, be insisting on some acceptance criteria

> There's no substitute for your own due dilligence...

of your own. A favourite is the obvious round-trip time for traffic.

After all, there's no point having a link between your Sheffield office and the provider's London point-of-presence if the round-trip time for the link between the two is over 80ms and thus way below what would normally constitute acceptable performance.

You can't be unreasonable and demand, say, 20ms latency between your Sheffield office and a cloud service based in New York (as Scotty would put it: "Ye cannae change the laws of physics") but if you're unsure of what's reasonable to expect, speak to your peers and ask them.

Acceptance criteria must be agreed

before you sign the contract. So think very hard about what you need, particularly if you're clouding client/server applications where link response and other performance metrics really matter.

In order to accept something you need it to have been delivered, so ensure you're clear on the delivery terms.

To consider one example, a service provider once had as part of its standard agreement, that penalties for late delivery of the new managed service ramped up from day zero to day 90. After that, they dropped off entirely, on the assumption that they'd deliver by then. So under, the terms of that agreement, they could have been 120 days late with little compensation.

SERVICE LEVEL

The concept of a Service Level Agreement (SLA) is very important. Suffice it to say, however, that you absolutely must have one either as part of, or directly referenced by, the main contract. You're putting your entire application in someone else's hands, and you must make damned sure that both parties agree about the level of service you're signing up to.

As we've already mentioned, you're right to expect the provider to be flexible and vary the terms. After all, what you're doing may well be unique or at least a variation on what they normally handle. So if there's something that you don't see you'd like to see specifically mentioned, ask for it to be included.

Don't be afraid to insist just because the service provider is much bigger than you. It's not unheard of for sizeable companies to say: "We've never had anyone ask for that before" and agree to include something, primarily because it clarified an otherwise ambiguous/unclear point.

On the other side of the coin, though, read what you do see and ask yourself whether you care that it's there. Many boiler-plate contracts are

> **Don't be afraid to insist just because the service provider is much bigger than you.**

catch-all documents that cover the service provider's range of services, not just the one(s) you're signing up for, and you can find yourself reading page 56 of an interminable document wondering whether a scary-looking clause applies to you. It can waste a lot of time and cause a great deal of unnecessary worry.

PRECEDENCE OF DOCUMENTS
It's very common for your contract to contain multiple documents.

A service agreement for a cloud service, for instance, could contain a master agreement that sits alongside no fewer than five additional documents – including the standard SLA, a separate document detailing the variations we insisted on to that SLA, the pricing schedule, and so on.

In any such arrangement, the master document must be explicit on the order of precedence of the various documents.

So, if you have variations to the standard SLA, ensure that it's clearly stated that your variations take precedence over the standard – otherwise your differences simply don't apply.

EXITING THE CONTRACT
You need to have a firm idea what will happen if you wish to leave that service provider.

What steps will be taken? Will you be able to get your data transferred within a particular time-frame? What if you're moving to another service provider – will the transfer be carried out smoothly?

This is a grey area as the whole cloud market is very new. There are no standard ways to proceed – in the way that customers can move between mobile providers via a PAC number for example.

It is very important this is considered from the outset and provisions are included in the contract.

LEGAL ASSISTANCE
It's idealistic to think contracts can be drawn up without a lawyer. A gentleman's handshake and all is fine but the world's not like that.

Lawyers are a necessary evil. Yes, they're expensive but, generally, jolly helpful.

Lawyers bring two things to the table. The obvious one is a collection of education or training that enables them to know about the law of contract, which can be a minefield but, in the average case, isn't.

Most contracts you'll enter into with service providers will be pretty simple law-wise – they'll state what you're responsible for and vice versa for the provider.

The most useful thing a lawyer brings you, though, is the fact that he or she has an innate compulsion to be a picky sod.

Your corporate lawyer, or your pet solicitor, is being paid to take as much notice of a sentence halfway down page 56 as the one at the beginning of page one. As such, they're likely to pick up on any issues that do exist.

If you're really blessed, you'll find a lawyer who has experience of the IT service industry - preferably the cloud implications of it.

This is because a lawyer without experience in this field will have a tendency to be very picky over items that they think suspicious but which are perfectly normal.

The usual one is the fact that some downtime is acceptable – that's anathema to your average lawyer who wants to slap a writ on the provider the moment they have scheduled downtime to upgrade.

It's a bit idealistic to think contracts can be drawn up without a lawyer.

A CONTRACT BY ANY OTHER NAME

The legalities of the contracts are largely the same as you'd have with any service provider.

Cover all the sensible eventualities and stick to your guns. Enlist help from others who can give firm, educated, enlightened guidance and almost certainly spot something you didn't.

Contract work needs to be carried out up-front. There is little opportunity for comeback after a system problem.

With cloud services it's important to make allowances for worst case scenarios. You should cover every eventuality in your contract and make sure it's as legally watertight as possible. ∎

■ CHAPTER 4 KEEPING THE BUSINESS RUNNING

Keep on running

One of the biggest concerns about running a business without a recognised IT department is what happens when things go wrong.

WITH THE HELP OF a manual and some handy work with Google, many small business owners and managers could run a basic system without calling on outside help. Or through judicious use of the right business partner, it is possible to run a slightly more advanced system.

But what happens when things go awry? After all, many of us have been confident enough to implement some technology only to panic when an unexpected error message appears – it's generally the excuse for some frantic switching on and off. It's a bit like using a phrase book to visit a foreign country. So far so good when everything goes according to plan, but all order is completely lost when something unexpected is said.

When you start dealing with computers, it can be like speaking a foreign language. There's new jargon to learn, a whole vocabulary of commands and, sometimes, there's no phrasebook to help you.

THERE MAY BE TROUBLE AHEAD

Running any type of business is fraught with challenges. Dealing with your IT problems is one of these. It's a challenge made harder by the lack of technical know-how. It's common for the reliance placed by small businesses on their IT infrastructure to be an order of magnitude greater than the internal expertise employed to fix those systems when they break.

> When you start dealing with computers, it can be like speaking a foreign language.

There's no short cut to making it easier. Apple likes to pretend that buying Macs is an easy way out – they're designed to be easy to use. This is true; they're a doddle – until things go wrong and then they're a big pain. Just talk to anyone who 'does' IT support within a large organisation. Most of them will tell you that when they don't work properly it's a whole different story – under-the-hood Mac diving is a non-trivial fix.

It's very important to note Apple is not the sole offender here. The trend within IT has been to make everything simpler to use. Indeed 20 years ago getting connected meant firing up a modem. This involved learning a whole new vocabulary and mastering the Hayes command set was like learning another language. In this era, running PCs meant knowing DOS inside out. Negotiating the internet in the pre-web days entailed ensuring you had a host of Unix commands at your fingertips.

MOVING FORWARD

A lot has changed since those days. Computers have become easier to use; connectivity has got simpler and software is easier to install. With its App Store, Apple hit upon a compelling truth – running apps doesn't have to be difficult. Furthermore, the emergence of Salesforce.com as a major player is a testament to the shift in power from IT departments to business users.

This commoditisation/consumerisation of IT has meant the landscape has changed completely. Any IT-confident halfwit can get a Windows server running with Active Directory and a bunch of domain-centric users, file shares and printers, but when something goes wrong, you'll end up reaching for the "Panic" button.

To deal with the issue you have two choices. One is to employ a skilled IT person to deal with all your potential issues, but this is expensive and you'll probably only need them for two or three days a year when something's gone

spectacularly pear-shaped. The other is to pay a third party to deal with your problems for you. In other words, you can move to the cloud.

Perhaps you don't want to move everything to the cloud. Indeed, perhaps you want to do something yourself or maybe one of your employees can be the part-time IT person. You need to examine your set-up and determine who can do what. You need to very carefully consider where can savings be made and decide on the most efficient way to proceed.

system. Modern stacking technologies make a set of switches into a single virtual device, and companies don't need techies with advanced networking qualifications to replace a device should one die. There are plenty of options available: the Cisco 3750 range is a very popular one, but there are much cheaper alternatives such as the GS752TXS from NetGear that also provides 48 Gigabit ports and high-speed stacking backplanes – more than enough for the average SMB. Just look around and see what's available, as it's a market that's changing all the time.

USER PCS

As with the office infrastructure, any employees are going to need computers. Unlike the office infrastructure, though, there is an opportunity to put some of their functionality in the cloud.

Consider the way one company

DISSECTING THE SMB

Let's look at different aspects of the small business infrastructure – some of which can be handled outside the company and some that needs to be handled in-house. Obviously, some of these don't apply to the one-person operation, but if you're running any type of small network, you need to look at these issues.

Structured cabling and LAN switches need to dealt with in situ. This could be problematical if you have no experience of networking although you could pay someone to manage these for you.

You may want to do it yourself. If so, you could over-provision the LAN switches so if a switch gets blown up it only affects a subset of the whole

With its App Store, Apple hit upon a compelling truth – running apps doesn't have to be difficult.

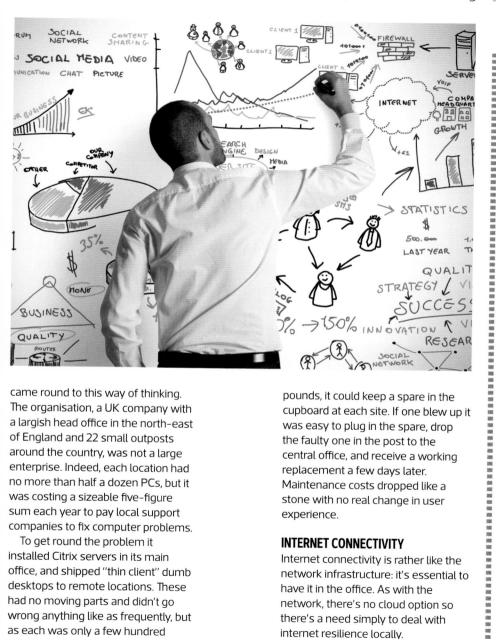

came round to this way of thinking. The organisation, a UK company with a largish head office in the north-east of England and 22 small outposts around the country, was not a large enterprise. Indeed, each location had no more than half a dozen PCs, but it was costing a sizeable five-figure sum each year to pay local support companies to fix computer problems.

To get round the problem it installed Citrix servers in its main office, and shipped "thin client" dumb desktops to remote locations. These had no moving parts and didn't go wrong anything like as frequently, but as each was only a few hundred pounds, it could keep a spare in the cupboard at each site. If one blew up it was easy to plug in the spare, drop the faulty one in the post to the central office, and receive a working replacement a few days later. Maintenance costs dropped like a stone with no real change in user experience.

INTERNET CONNECTIVITY

Internet connectivity is rather like the network infrastructure: it's essential to have it in the office. As with the network, there's no cloud option so there's a need simply to deal with internet resilience locally.

As with most technologies, it can be done expensively or cheaply. It's possible to have internet connections that require reasonable-spec routers to talk BGP with service providers upstream, if a company needs this level of robustness and functionality. There are, however, also far lower-cost alternatives like entry-level firewall-routers, such as the DrayTek DSL router, that have dual WAN ports.

Web servers are another matter. It's an easy option to host websites in the cloud – in fact, it's a deployment that makes perfect sense as it allows you to cope with unexpected peaks and troughs without the need to over-provision a web server.

APPLICATION PROVISION

When it comes to applications, we're firmly back in the comfort zone of the cloud providers. This is very much a how-long-is-a-piece-of-string question. The obvious first step is to move email to the cloud, but there really isn't any reason not to 'cloud' many of the apps that are being run within the organisation.

> Maintenance costs dropped like a stone with no real change in user experience.

Step one is the browser-based stuff (users really won't notice the difference with apps like Oracle Financials when they're moved to the cloud, so long as the connectivity is reasonably fast) but it may be better to bite the bullet and adopt a thin client desktop strategy so the whole lot can be put in a the cloud – either in a private cloud or a SaaS model.

SERVERS

What about the servers needed to run the business? If apps are being moved into the cloud then there will be no need to run the servers they were working on, but there's still a nucleus of servers that will need to be retained in-house: directory services, file services and print services are the main three.

The initial problem to overcome is that the servers need to exist in the first place. Second is the fact that file servers, in particular, will be slower when placed at the other end of a wide-area link. Be a bit constructive, though, and some of it can be moved into the cloud – the key to this approach is the introduction of WAN optimisers within your business.

That sounds complicated but WAN optimisation is the name given to a series of techniques that aims to improve the way in which data is handled from outside your premises. It can work by compressing data or by de-duplication (both of these techniques involve reducing the volume of data that is being sent) or by latency optimisation (i.e. cutting down the distance data has to travel).

Run WAN optimisation over an IPSec link through a decent internet connection and users won't notice the file server is actually a couple of hundred miles away in a data centre.

You don't need to know the ins and outs of these technologies, you just need to know they are viable options.

TELECOMS

The final office function many companies rely on hugely is telephony. Although it's possible to use mobiles if phones are down, this is a pain and it's a non-trivial task to get inbound calls re-routed.

Sadly, the range of hosted telephony offerings is still very limited. There are services like Vonage but they're not really 'proper' telephony. But, if there isn't a decent cloud service, IP telephony is a reasonable option.

Many apparently proprietary handsets can also play at being SIP clients, for instance, and it's possible to introduce virtualisation to make life easier. That is, until the world wakes up and give us widespread, full-service VoIP hosting.

Most business activities can, however, be placed in the cloud for someone else to manage. Servers, apps and telephony all work in either the private or public cloud - the latter depends on location and what different suppliers offer.

TROUBLESHOOTING

These are just some of the factors to

This is very much a how-long-is-a-piece-of-string type question.

consider. There are plenty of choices available for organisations that are not looking for on-premise options.

The traditional approach, which has been going on since Mark Zuckerberg was in short trousers, is to pay a

consultant or support company a retainer to monitor systems and be available for call-outs when something needs hands-on attention.

There are plenty of consultants who make a nice living from this kind of user support and it does work very well in the average case. It's particularly useful when that organisation can sit between you and the more useless of the IT service providers you deal with.

While many people who work for service providers are excellent, some of them are lacking on decent technical support. It's a sad fact of life.

It's easy to tell the ones who have little understanding. They follow a script and suggest solutions that are totally inappropriate. For example, it's not unknown for these companies to report that the problem is lying with your Outlook Express settings – even if you don't use Outlook Express.

That's why moving away from PCs in the workplace is such a winner. If you move to cloud-based servers and thin client devices on people's desks the entire support task is consolidated to two simple processes: (1) if the desktop device dies, get the spare one out of the cupboard and post the broken one to head office and (2) if the UK-wide network dies, call the service provider.

The chances are that all but the smallest of businesses will have some kind of internal technical expertise – and if not, it may be time to appoint one of your employees as the go-to IT man or woman.

You don't want to dispose of this

> ## There are plenty of consultants who make a nice living from this kind of user support.

internal capability completely, because, as mentioned earlier, there will always be technical challenges that need an on-site person with an element of IT capability if they're to be solved in a timely fashion and with appropriate timeliness and diligence.

The answer's pretty obvious, then: play to that individual's talents and outsource the more complex aspects to cloud setups.

If you do this, then, what type of internal ability do you need?

BASIC DIAGNOSTICS

If you buy managed services from a third party and something isn't working, you need someone who can

understand where the problem may lie. This doesn't mean they know how to fix it (the system may be opaque, so this may be impossible) but it does mean that, for example, in a cloud-based app that you access via the internet, your tech staff can say with a reasonable level of confidence whether the issue is local, internet-related or part of the managed service. This general diagnostic capability is the top requirement, since in some cases they will have to speculate or extrapolate to consider services whose innards aren't immediately visible.

VENDOR MANAGEMENT

When you outsource your services, you need someone who can liaise effectively with the vendor both on a day-to-day basis and when the chips are down. Standard vendor management isn't the rocket science people make it out to be (an SLA is an SLA, and generally they're written in words that even the lawyer signing the contract will understand). What matters most is the relationship when something's down.

You need someone who is firm but fair, who cajoles rather than rants, and who raises highest priority faults as high priority and low priority faults as low priority instead of expecting urgency for the slightest glitch. A similar approach is required for security. Elements that don't need to be high security (i.e there's no sensitive data) should not be.

When the vendor has been engaged to assist with a problem, the on-site techie needs to swallow his or her pride and be a pair of "intelligent hands" for the vendor's team as the latter try to diagnose the problem.

Even if you think you know better, you need to bow down to the vendor engineers because they may well know a great deal more about the setup than you do. Given the inflated ego of many techies this can actually be something of a wrench, but it's an absolutely essential ingredient since there are times - annoyingly - that you will need to defer to someone else's superior knowledge.

A HEALTHY CYNICISM

Ultimately, though, you must have someone with a brain who can see through all the noise and air-headedness and know when to escalate with the vendor in order to get to a timely fix. There are countless examples in recent years where the vendor techie has sounded plausible but something's just sounded wrong, whether it be that they've misunderstood something or that, in one case, they've been looking at the wrong diagram and are tweaking someone else's installation.

Solving technical problems in a small business in the modern day is, then, a combination of adopting vendor services such that you don't need super-specialist internal IT staff and then employing sufficient in-house capabilities to enable you to

PROFIT RISK LOSS

Ultimately, you must have someone with a brain who can see through the noise and air-headedness and know when to escalate with the vendor.

manage those suppliers, understand the end-to-end service at a technical level, maintain the service levels that you need, and work together to resolve the issues that will, inevitably, crop up from time to time.

This chapter cannot begin to resolve all your problems for you. As we mentioned right at the start, you may think you have everything under control and then something unexpected happens. Have a word with an IT support person of some years experience and most of them will tell that even after 20 years of grunt work, they still come across new problems.

There are many ways in which computers can go wrong and when that propensity for error is multiplied by problems with networks and software, you might as well be exploring a whole new world.

It should be observed that 99.9 per cent of all computers will work fine for 99.9 per cent of the time though. By a judicious mixture of your own IT expertise, help from cloud providers and occasional consultation with Mr Google, you should be able to run your own business without a dedicated IT department, yet be able to call on a variety of different applications and technologies.

Cloud brings the power of the enterprise to the smallest business and now is the time to make full use of the possibilities. ∎

Keeping email running

Email is one of the simpler moves you can make to the cloud. Before you make the jump, though, you need to choose a service. And to choose a service, you need to have a list of requirements so you know what to look for.

MALWARE/AV/SPAM INSPECTION

Inbound inspection is a necessity and outbound inspection is at the very least a should have. Central system control must be via an interface that's accessible by support staff. A user-facing self-service portal is a very nice touch too.

DIRECTORY SYNC/INTEGRATION

It's absolutely unacceptable for your email user database not to be synchronised with your general LAN user database. Email is crucial to your organisation, and if you have separate logins for your email system you risk not only widespread user dissatisfaction but also, more importantly, users' email accounts persisting when they leave the organisation.

CALENDARS AND CONTACTS

You'll want seamless ability to send and receive meeting invitations, check invitees' availability and accept/reject invitations with a single click, so it makes sense to use a calendar system that's integrated with the email engine.

COST MODEL

Be careful to understand the cost model and what you get for your money.

Don't unwittingly fall for a free/cheap service only to realise later that once you go above a modest storage limit the charges ramp up like a mountain range. Understand whether the cost is based on storage, user count or both, and be clear on termination conditions.

DESKTOP CLIENT

Although the email core is in the cloud, your users will still want to be able to use desktop client applications. The obvious choice is Microsoft Outlook, though of course Lotus Notes is in there too.

SMARTPHONE CLIENT

You will almost certainly want them to be able to work with email on their phones. Smartphones all have native email clients that can interact via proprietary protocols or open standards.

SECURE WEBMAIL

Webmail is an obvious inclusion, but some companies don't like it for security reasons. Webmail's as secure as you make it, though, so if you're nervous about allowing access to confidential material with a simple password you have the option to add multi-factor authentication.

■ CHAPTER 5 SECURITY

Security for small businesses

How can you employ the virtual equivalent of big, burly bouncers to safeguard your small, but oh so important, tech assets?

SO FAR, WE'VE LOOKED at many of the advantages of cloud computing and the ways in which a small business can bring the power of the enterprise to its modest concern.

But for most people who have looked at cloud computing, there's one overwhelming problem: how secure is it? It's this issue that caused many companies to look askance at cloud; how can you trust a third-party to look after your data and protect the integrity of your company? It's an issue that worries many enterprises – who often have the benefit of a full-time security officer – so it terrifies many small businesses.

There are two concerns here: one is the problem faced by every company – how to keep your systems safe in the face of an onslaught from hackers, phishers, virus writers, identity fraudsters and every form of cyber criminal under the sun. And the problem faced solely by companies that have entrusted stuff to cloud providers – how do you ensure that their systems are secure, that they will look after your data and they can keep the bad guys at bay.

The first thing to point out is that cloud service providers are generally pretty good at keeping systems secure. It is after all their bread and butter – a service provider that is hacked regularly won't really be getting many customers. The level of security expertise they have tends to be far higher than that of the average company and it's certainly going to be higher than that of a small business, particularly one that's not especially blessed with technical know-how (and that's most of them).

ALL ABOUT TRUST

Although it seems that trusting a third-party is risky, we do it all the time. How many thousands of us have bank accounts that can be accessed online? We're clearly ready to trusts our banks to have our best interests at heart. More appropriately, how many of us are content to leave our credit card details with Amazon? Millions of people across the world do – and Amazon is one of the major cloud providers. Admittedly the Amazon retail division and its cloud subsidiary are very different but we are ready to trust that the company culture is geared towards security.

There's a concern that small businesses have less to worry about when it comes to security, they have less to steal than the banks and the

large companies but this is a misguided view.

But those who may think computer security is a low priority, ask yourself this: Would you leave the doors to your uninsured office unlocked and the windows wide open, hoping the robbers didn't notice? Of course not, but many small companies do fail to consider their security needs.

The casual cyber criminal is oblivious to business size; they're simply looking for a security hole through which to climb. Cyber crime is

Coopers Information Security Breaches Survey 2012, 76 per cent of small business suffered a security breach the previous year. Breaking those figures down further; 15 per cent of small businesses suffered a denial of service attack, while 20 per cent of these SMBs lost confidential data. The price of these breaches can be devastating. Some 70 per cent of companies experiencing a major data loss go out of business within a year.

While it's easy to get worried about faceless hackers and cyber criminals sitting in Russian apartments, don't forget the danger from your own company: there are many internal threats too: users accidentally deleting large chunks of data; a virus infecting a laptop, which goes on to hit your network; a disenchanted employee doing deliberate damage.

Bearing this in mind, the most worrying statistic of all is that only 22 per cent of small businesses back up data on a daily basis and 55 per cent don't have a formal disaster recovery plan – figures that should ring alarm bells in the minds of all small business managers.

MALWARE THREATS

New malware is released and new vulnerabilities discovered with alarming regularity. In the last quarter of 2012 alone, an average of 2.5 million online threats were detected every month, according to the latest McAfee Threats Report.

Be it malware infection, identity

> ## Ask yourself this: Would you leave the doors to your uninsured office unlocked?

well-organised and highly automated, with bots running scans for security vulnerabilities across the internet, and others ready to exploit them with devastating implications for the SMB.

According to Price Waterhouse

theft through phishing and social engineering, ever improving password-cracking technologies or sloppy coding leading to exploitable vulnerabilities in software, the type of threats you're exposed to is evolving fast and unpredictably.

Factor in the accidental impact of your employees knowing just enough about technology to be dangerous (copying data to a USB stick for some at home working, using business resources to visit high-risk websites, installing software they use at home which might inadvertently compromise your business security) and the threat landscape broadens even more.

Indeed, the security threat landscape can best be summed up in two words: dangerously dynamic.

WHAT CAN BE DONE?

For any company, be it a two person operation or a huge international corporation, securing their data is one of the key areas they have to look at when it comes to effectively running their business.

What makes the small business different to the enterprise, however, is it will often not have an internal IT department, or even one person responsible for the computers.

This is not necessarily a bad thing. Outsourcing IT can leave SMBs, in particular, freer to concentrate on

> The price of these breaches can be devastating. Some 70 per cent of companies experiencing a major data loss go out of business within a year.

day-to-day operations.

Even if IT is outsourced, these smaller companies still need to be aware of the dangers posed by cyber crime, such as hacking and malware, and be able to defend themselves against it.

According to Carl Leonard, senior manager at Websense Security Labs, the threats faced by small businesses are "remarkably similar" to those faced by larger enterprises.

"Small businesses can embrace the web just as much as anyone [but] with this comes exposure to social media threats, mobile threats and targeted attacks," says Leonard.

"It is not necessarily the number of employees or revenue generated that dictates a company's exposure, but the quality of data that lies behind their network perimeter. Malware authors are after that data," he added.

SMBs can face the same threats as enterprises, but without having the inside knowledge to fend them off, they may be lacking the ability to defend themselves.

"Small businesses face malware threats on two fronts, which spreads their often limited resources even thinner," says Marcin Kleczynski, CEO and founder of anti-malware vendor Malwarebytes.

"Firstly, there are the mass market consumer/small business malware such as rogue

applications, which are increasingly prevalent amongst both small businesses and consumers alike. Secondly, small businesses have to be aware of the more targeted threats. Many think these are the preserve of large corporations, but there are many cyber criminals who make a good living out of just targeting smaller companies," Kleczynski says.

The fact that SMBs typically have to

> The security threat landscape can be best summed up in two words: dangerously dynamic.

face these threats without dedicated IT resources or with minimal security expertise can compound their effects, he adds.

All is not lost for SMBs, however. There are many ways in which these companies can protect themselves and their customers from the attacks launched against them by cyber criminals.

Rik Ferguson, vice president of security research at Trend Micro, advises seeking outside help.

"[As having internal IT support becomes rarer], there is an increasingly large number of security partners or resellers out there who are offering managed and hosted services for exactly this type of SMB customer," he says.

Ferguson explained that this kind of offering allows the security partner of choice to remotely manage and monitor the client SMB's IT for any threats or breaches.

"With this type of arrangement, everybody benefits – the small business gets the benefits ... having an IT department looking after things for them, without the related staffing costs. The security partners benefit from not having to travel anywhere near as much in order to make sure their customers are ok – they will only

> Without having the inside knowledge to fend attacks off, they may be lacking the ability to defend themselves.

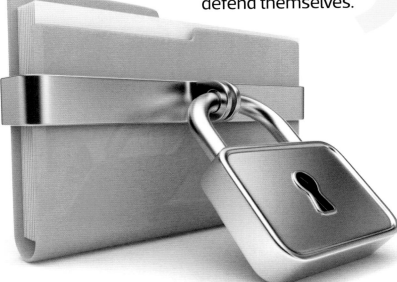

Dos and Don'ts of security

DO

 Implement a security policy and ensure all your staff – with NO exceptions – follow it

 Set an example by following safe practice at all times

 Encrypt everything that's confidential

 Ask your service provider detailed questions about its own practices

 Take data protection laws seriously – the authorities have teeth

DON'T

 Take security for granted

 Think that because you're small no-one is interested in you

 Think there's such a thing as a one-size fits all security policy

 Assume that everyone knows about security policies, drum it into them

---

need to go to a site if a problem cannot be resolved through the hosted management interface," he adds.

Kleczynski has also noticed this trend. "We see that more small businesses are looking for IT and security management platform partners, or managed service providers (MSPs), (which) leverage a platform such as Kaseya or Continuum," he says.

However, just bringing in a security partner is not enough, small businesses need to be taking a layered approach to security. "There has to be a combination of people, processes and technology," says Leonard. "Without a dedicated captain

at the helm, or help in the form of an IT team, the users should be educated so that they have a better chance of noticing a threat, should they see one.

"Furthermore, small businesses should put their trust in technology. Companies can buy into intelligence, expertise and advanced technologies that would otherwise cost hundreds of millions to configure and maintain."

Kleczynski too believes technology is an important weapon. "We have always been advocates of including [malware detection and prevention] technologies alongside that of traditional antivirus technologies," he says. "It is a bit like making sure a car has seatbelts AND airbags."

However, Ferguson adds that, while

it is important to build these preventative 'walls', all companies of all sizes must adjust their thinking to "accept the reality of compromise" and build 'inside out security'.

"We previously always used to protect from the outside in – build a strong perimeter and build layers inwards to the centre of the network," Ferguson says. Now, however, he believes companies must start from the assumption that they will be breached and build defences from the inside out to prevent them from leaving with the data they came for – what he describes as 'building a deeper dungeon'.

But what if, as an SMB, you don't just want to get rid of the need for an IT department? What if you want to get rid of your IT infrastructure altogether and move to the cloud?

Trade body the Cloud Industry Forum has gone so far as to set up a special interest group to look into the issue of security and the cloud.

Yet according to Leonard, the cloud can actually help SMBs to enhance their overall security.

"Cloud technology can be an easy way [for small businesses] to access security technologies that would otherwise be prohibitive without an in-house IT team," he says.

"If your data is hosted in the cloud, use Data Loss Prevention products to ensure your data is being sent to your cloud vendor and not a compromised server," he adds.

Ferguson goes further, stating "encryption is really the only thing you can rely on in the cloud.

"If your data is hosted with a cloud service, you are not going to have access to the low-level auditing and access logs you normally would to reassure yourself there was no inappropriate accessing of it," he says.

"So you should be able to provision that data encrypted to your cloud

> ## The cloud can actually help SMBs to enhance their overall security.

provider, you need to be able to retain management of the encryption keys to ensure your cloud provider is not inappropriately accessing your data, and you need to make sure that those keys are available to applications that deal with your data. Encryption is your primary, if not your only, weapon to ensure confidentiality and integrity of data in somebody else's environment."

ENCRYPTION

Businesses wanting to stay secure have several options but encryption is certainly going to play its part.

But what is encryption? For most people, it's geekdom personified, a real-life manifestation of higher mathematics. And as such, it's something that will scare just about everyone who's not an über-geek.

There's no doubt that encryption is one of the dark arts. Which shouldn't be too surprising as that's the whole point: encryption transforms data using a cipher in order to make it unreadable to anyone without the key that unscrambles it.

This notion of scrambling data goes back at least as far as Ancient Greece when the Spartans used something called a Scytale, a wooden cylinder around which a piece of parchment was wrapped and a message written across it. That message made no sense when the parchment was unwound, only becoming clear again when wrapped around another scytale of the same size.

Fast forward two thousand years and all that has really changed is that we've introduced computers, where ciphers are now the algorithms that scramble the data and the scytales have turned into the 'keys' we use on our computers to unlock, or decrypt, that encrypted data.

In this day and age, data encryption is ubiquitous. Buying something online with a credit card? That transaction will be encrypted by one of two technologies: Transport Layer Security (TLS) or Secure Sockets Layer (SSL). Use a wireless router to access the internet? That will probably use Wi-Fi Protected Access II (WPA2) to prevent unauthorised access by others. Keep a backup of important or confidential data on a USB memory stick or removable hard drive? Then let's hope it would be encrypted in case of loss or theft.

If you're using the cloud then you're going to be using one of the techniques mentioned above.

The cloud sounds a bit detached from some of those examples but think of it as being as giant storage device and all of a sudden storing such data without proper encryption enters the realms of madness.

Yet that madness not only exists, it exists within enterprises large and small as demonstrated by the number of data breach stories to have hit the headlines over the last couple of years, any of which could have been prevented if only the data itself had been encrypted.

So how can you ensure that you're not going to see your company making the headlines in your local newspaper?

We can't go into the finer details of encryption here – there are plenty of resources available if you want to make a deep dive into the technology.

However, what you can take on board is that if you want to beef up your company's security, you need to be asking the right questions of your service provider.

There are two questions to ask: will my data be encrypted in transit? (the answer will almost certainly be 'yes' – if not, time to move on the next service provider) and will my data be encrypted at rest? This is a much more important question to ask.

If the answer to this question is 'no' then your choice is to walk away and find another service provider or to encrypt the data before it leaves your own office. But if the answer is 'yes' then there's a follow-up question: who holds the encryption keys?

This is something that's often overlooked, but shouldn't be undervalued. If you adhere to the assumption that encryption capability of your CSP must match the importance/confidentiality of the data being stored, then handing over possession of the keys to access that data to the CSP could be asking for trouble. Not only could you be at risk from unwanted access but, if you're a business in regulated environment, you

So how can you ensure that you're not going to see your company making the headlines in your local newspaper?

could come under fire from industry compliance officers.

If you don't want to risk your data in the cloud, then it's possible to store your data and manage your encryption. This leaves you with the responsibility of looking after your encryption keys. All well and good but if you lose them, well, then you're screwed.

Whatever choice you make, you need to think very carefully about who has the keys and who has access to your data. It could be the difference between your company surviving and your company thriving.

DATA PROTECTION

Every now and then, a security breach makes the headlines. The most notable one in the UK was when the Inland Revenue 'lost' the details of seven million taxpayers. There

are strict regulations in place to protect data and while it's the big organisations like the Inland Revenue that make the headlines, the guidelines apply to all companies, big and small.

The data protection regulations, which apply to information collected and processed on individuals, and which, of course, are applicable to any computer systems, cloud or non-cloud. Among the key principles of the Data Protection Act are those that relate to security:

- **Appropriate technical and organisational measures shall be taken against unauthorised or unlawful processing of personal data.**
- **Personal data shall not be transferred to a country or territory outside the European Economic Area unless that country or territory ensures an adequate level of protection for the rights and freedoms of data subjects in relation to the processing of personal data.**

So while there is no prohibition of using a cloud provider that may have data centres outside of the UK or European Union – as many do – it may be very difficult to know exactly where a copy of data may be in a rapidly changing commercial environment, and what local regulations may apply in countries where data is physically held.

In the code on protecting personal data issued by the Information Commissioner's Office, there is a section on operating internationally that includes advice on cloud computing. It states:

"The Data Protection Act does not prohibit the overseas transfer of personal data, but it does require that it is protected adequately wherever it is located and whoever is processing it. Clearly, this raises compliance issues that firms using internet-based computing need to address.

"Your use of an internet-based service must not lead you to relinquish control of the personal data you have collected, or expose it to security risks that would not have arisen had the data remained in your possession in the UK. There must be a written contract in place. This can be an electronic one, requiring the internet-based service provider to only act on your instructions and to have a level of security equivalent to yours."

Things can get very complicated if you are holding data about people from many different countries, as there may be cultural differences in what is deemed acceptable to collect and store, but the code does say that the UK Act has international roots and is a good foundation for widespread compliance.

Those organisations that hold highly sensitive data such as personal health records and customer credit cards will probably not want to commit them to a international public cloud provider for applications such as storage and commerce – and the DPA does also make specific reference to a category of 'sensitive data', especially about personal matters, which must be protected.

BYOD

Everyone seems to have a smartphone or a tablet these days and your staff will probably want to start using theirs in the office. They'd be following a trend: according to research company Gartner, by 2014 about 80 per cent of professionals will use at least two personal devices to in the workplace

This means that your company's security, previously thought to be near-watertight, will now have a new element of risk. It is crucial that the key 'housekeeping' issues are understood within organisations. When in 2012 Osterman Research surveyed more than 100 SMB IT security providers on behalf of Trend Micro, it confirmed that the BYOD trend was on the up

amongst SMBs.

Trend Micro noted at the time that the typical SMB employee uses a whole raft of BYOD endpoint devices, and these need to be properly secured if the business is to be protected from exposure to malware and other threats. Which begs the question, just how does the average SMB go about translating security concerns into real-world policies in the face of the BYOD flood?

Although you may think that's it's not feasible to restrict your employees to only using a particular flavour of the Android OS on a specific hardware platform, and such an extreme is unlikely to be workable, that's not actually the case.

What you can do is recommend devices which you are able to support from the data security perspective, such as iPhones and iPads running iOS version 'x' or later and hardware running Android version whatever. If you say what you can support, by implication it means you can also state anything else is not supported and therefore must not be used to access or store corporate data.

The same 'say what' approach is much harder to extend to software and services if employees want to use their own devices. Some SMBs will attempt to go down the policy road of banning Twitter and Facebook apps, third party email clients or VPNs for example, on the basis that these apps may have security vulnerabilities

> ## Your company's security, previously thought to be near–watertight, will now have an element of risk.

which could impact upon data.

The fact of the matter is that it's all but impossible to police such a policy and prevent such apps from being installed and used. It's also a fact, unfortunately, that the bad guys do see consumer-grade apps as being a route to stealing business data.

Any BYOD security policy is, therefore, better directed at bridging the security time gap. This can be best thought of as being the time between malware being released and protection against it being deployed. Policy should wrap with technology

How does the average SMB go about translating security concerns into real-world policies in the face of the BYOD flood?

here, and the SMB should look to implementing as near as possible, a real time approach to security pattern/signature updates. The cloud can help, with an increasing number of threat intelligence and pattern updating products being available now that both save on endpoint resources and remediate newly launched threats quickly.

Your policy has to be something of a balancing act between the fact that the devices it applies to are not company property, but at the same time are being used to access company data. This inevitably is going to involve compromise, much of it from the employee side of the fence.

A BYOD policy shouldn't just cover data security, it should also embrace general usage. Your Acceptable Use Policy (AUP) and your BYOD policy should be joined at the hip, ensuring that unacceptable activities are not

enabled courtesy of an employee using a smartphone instead of the desktop or company laptop.

This may seem straightforward, but the question of monitoring and enforcement may not be and legal advice is always recommended before considering using any such monitoring tools available to you.

What happens when an employee is no longer an employee? Obviously you wouldn't want them to still be able to access your company data, but you cannot just confiscate their iPhone when they leave.

Your policy should cover the enforced removal of company data, security tokens and so on. If you decide to take the 'exit wipe' route, then you had better also consider how you back up their personal data so that can be reinstalled after the company stuff has been wiped.

Talking of wiping of a device, the data storage should be included in your BYOD policy. Data segregation is the accepted norm, with a distinct system in place to ensure business and personal data is separated.

There should also be systems in place to automate data back-ups, external to the device itself with the cloud being the obvious answer, and an agreed method of dealing with data in the event of the device being lost or stolen.

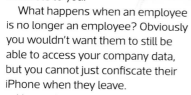

The bad guys do see consumer-grade apps as being a route to stealing business data.

Once you have a policy in place, it should not be considered a cast-iron solution to BYOD security. Your policy needs to be audited regularly to ensure any new loopholes are uncovered and patched quickly. An out-of-date policy is worse than having no policy at all; a false sense of security leaves the potential data breach door wide open.

There is no such thing as a one-size-fits-all BYOD policy. The policy isn't the be all and end all of BYOD security, it's just a part in the overall puzzle. Ensure you also educate users and complement efforts with solid tech solutions. ∎

CHAPTER 6 MANAGING COSTS

Keeping an eye on the bank balance

Look after the pennies and the pounds will look after themselves, right? Regardless of whether you're big or small, you have to keep an eye on costs.

THREE OR FOUR YEARS ago, it was very clear what the main driver was for cloud computing: the need to bring down costs.

It was the aftermath of the financial crash, when companies were faced with a credit squeeze and when public sector organisations felt the full force of budget cuts. In such circumstances, it was obvious why cloud was used to drive down costs. Here was a way to pay for what was being used – and only for what was being used. No longer would there be a need to over-provision IT services and pay for redundant computing power.

It saved money but there was also the issue of accounting for cloud services. Because buying cloud was based on a monthly subscription or for what was being used, there was no longer a need to find the cash up-front. In other words, there had been a shift from capital expenditure (Cap-Ex) to operational expenditure (Op-Ex).

However, small businesses should be wary of moving to cloud and automatically saving money – while in most cases it will be a way to keep costs down, nothing in life is certain and cloud could end up costing more.

But the overwhelming trend is for cloud to be a cost-saver. A survey from IDC released in July 2012, found that companies moving to cloud can expect some considerable cost savings – a figure of 600 per cent saving was quoted. While that sort of figure may be exceptional, the norm is certainly that cloud will save money – but to do so needs some planning.

Part of the problem is that shifting to cloud is a completely different way to do business and it can be hard to align costs properly purely because some applications are being handled completely differently. It's certainly not unknown for the first-time cloud user to be faced with some unexpectedly high bills. The reasons could vary. These increased costs could be from demand spikes caused by higher than expected use of apps or denial of service attacks, to virtual machines that don't get turned off after use; though poor capacity planning comes in many guises.

RESOURCE OPTIMISATION

It is here that the inexperienced companies can come unstuck. Most problems are not with Software-as-a-Service (SaaS) implementations but with cloud infrastructures. If you're running a business without specialist

networking staff, then it may well be best to get some help here as the problems can be quite specialised. They include factors such as poor load-balancing or auto-scaling.

All is not lost, however. Your service provider should offer tools to help you manage this. But these only go so far. You would be well advised to turn to a new generation of cloud analytic providers who can supply software tools that help non-IT specialists monitor, manage and even dynamically optimise cloud resources. Some of the more sophisticated can help ascertain detailed IT resource use – whether it's in the cloud or part of your on-premise infrastructure.

Tools available to do this include Cloudyn, a start-up and one of the growing band of providers specialising in cloud usage analytics (others include NewVem and Cloud Cruiser). Certainly, an inexperienced user will benefit from judicious application of some of these specialist tools.

There's another way to keep costs down and that's by advantage of the reserved instances offered by some cloud providers to reduce overheads - these enable long-term users to benefit from discounts.

Reserved instances can offer assured capacity availability and cost savings on the AWS on-demand instances, but reserved instance contracts range from one to three years, so weighing up the trade off between costs and utilisation and

Part of the problem is that shifting to the cloud is a completely different way to do business.

between flexibility and a long-term commitment is a challenge.

AWS also offers a third possibility; there is a Spot Instance option where potential customers can bid for unused Amazon capacity. Customers set the maximum price they're prepared to pay and if their bid exceeds the current spot price then their order is fulfilled.

It is certainly worth exploring all the

> If you're running a business without specialist networking staff, then it may be best to get some help.

possibilities available to you. Just as many householders find themselves tied to inappropriate energy tariffs, so can companies find themselves paying too much for cloud services: companies that are not heavy users of Amazon services, for example, could opt for Light Utilisation Reserved Instances and save themselves a heap of money. It's certainly worth shopping around.

CAPEX AND OPEX

It's taken as read that services purchased as part of capital expenditure are a bad thing and those that are OpEx acquisitions are a good thing. However, this is rather simplistic from an accountant's point of view. While it's true that OpEx is convenient shorthand for 'day-to-day operating expenses', the definition of CapEx is not quite so straightforward.

At its most basic, CapEx refers to the expenses that a business incurs when it invests in new 'assets' or existing ones, but this simplistic explanation hides layers of complexity. The accounting definition, classification, guidelines, scope and implications of CapEx all vary depending on context. There are also issues such as tangible and intangible assets, their depreciation and amortisation, accounting for different national tax jurisdictions, and capital lease arrangements to consider.

It's a finely nuanced argument because financing access to IT expenditure is not just a matter of shifting to OpEx, the decision could have an impact on another part of the business – it could have an impact on small business' tax burden, for example, and robbing the Peter of capital expenditure to pay the Paul of

HMRC may not be the best thing to do. The question a business has to ask itself is it better to pay out now or pay out over the next year or next three years? The answer may be "Yes" but beware that such a decision could be regretted when the tax bills come around.

However, some things *are* straightforward. Buying SaaS should always be financed as part of the operational budget – there's no clear benefit here of considering such purchases as part of CapEx.

For more complex decisions, however, it's important to involve your accountant make sure that you're minimising your tax burden, while also ensuring that you're getting the best possible equipment and software for your business.

CAN YOU DO IT FOR FREE?

If you're running a small business, the cost of the applications you need in order to run it properly can soak up a significant chunk of your profits. Yet there's absolutely no reason that you can't trim this cost to the bone by a little judicious use of free software, with a hefty chunk of cloud in there for good measure.

There are three primary components in the toolbox you'll need to run your business:

■ **General tools that most businesses would need, such as office applications and email.**
■ **Tools that you need for the**

back-office tasks – paying your taxes, producing invoices, CRM and banking.
■ **Specialist tools that are specific to your particular business.**

If you want a completely free office application suite, the place to start is OpenOffice, which is now part of the Apache family. Despite being free it has all the features you'd need in an office suite, and they're all properly fully-featured. Most companies use MS Office - and that's what people are used to - but OpenOffice contains

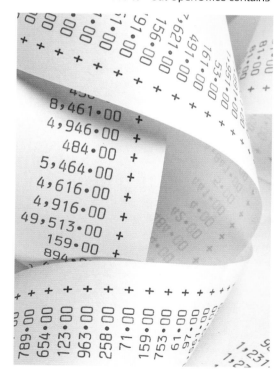

everything that MS Office does (and runs on Macs too) and once you've got used to the GUI differences it works a treat.

OpenOffice is not a cloud-based app range – though it is multi-platform. If you want to take a cloud option then you'll have to live with a modest cost – though given what you get it really is very inexpensive indeed. A company could survive quite easily on OpenOffice – just bear in mind that while it can read Microsoft files, it doesn't work in reverse so if you're dealing with a company that's a heavy Microsoft user, it may have difficulty reading the stuff you send it.

The two options you'll consider are Google Apps (at £3.30 per user per month for the basic package) or

Most companies use Microsoft Office and that's what people are used to.

Microsoft Office at a tenner a month. Is the Google option sufficient for the average small business? Yes, probably. On the other hand, the Microsoft option is what you're probably more used to so it's a question of whether familiarity is worth seven quid a month to you.

Note that email has not been considered as part of the above – it's an entirely separate concept. There's really only one choice here: Google.

It's something that's easy to use, is reliable – even with multiple company addresses – and doesn't cost a bean. It can be used with a web interface and with an IMAP client (Thunderbird – which is free, of course) and they work just great.

Small businesses can benefit from a lot of free software and websites that can help with tax matters. Aside from any filing fees there's no cost for doing your company returns online, and small business owners can rely on HMRC's cool tools to manage the

PAYE (tax and National Insurance) calculations each month. It's possible to do quarterly VAT returns using an OpenOffice spreadsheet, and the bank's web banking site can help here too. You can spend hundreds or even thousands on business packages, and there really isn't a need.

For your invoicing needs, BillFaster is free in its basic form, though as with many zero-cost online solutions you may find that you want to spend a few quid a month on some of the chargeable, more advanced features.

Getting a handle on the money side of things

There are no set rules for managing costs within a small business but here's some general guidance.

DO

 Plan ahead – you need a resource provisioning policy

 Monitor service usage to prevent budget overruns

 Control storage costs – duplicate, idle and unknown files cost money

 Dynamically optimise resource use to exploit new pricing plans and service options

 Scale up monitoring and management to reflect increased cloud resource use

DON'T

 Underestimate the complexity of pricing plans and service options

 Miss out on the opportunity to cut costs by using cloud more efficiently

 Take a one-size-fits-all approach – match public cloud instances to need

 Run more instances than necessary

 Leave virtual machines running when not in use

> Small businesses can benefit from a lot of free software and websites that can help with tax matters.

Do you need to do this? Probably not – you can just use a spreadsheet template in OpenOffice, for instance, and export the results as PDFs. Again not in the cloud, but sometimes you want to have your data on your stand-alone laptop and not rely on being connected to the world 24/7.

Finally, if your customer base is too big to handle with a simple database, you can look to cloud-based CRM systems for managing client information. FreeCRM is the place to start in this respect; although chargeable in its larger forms, you can have up to 10 users for free.

With both your business apps and your back-office operations, you need to be mindful of the requirement for backups (particularly if you use a non-cloud office suite). There are several free cloud back-up services, but to pick three major ones, check out iDrive, which offers 5GB free, Microsoft's SkyDrive, which provides 7GB of free storage and Google Drive which also offers 5GB free. The free "starter" storage levels will quickly fill up though and there's a charge for more if you need it.

The place where costs can spiral is in the applications that are specific to what you do. Technical specialists are

The Cloud.
Distilled.

Everything you need to know about how cloud computing will change your business

www.cloudpro.co.uk

used to getting umpty-squillion free tools for everything from terminal emulation to infrastructure monitoring. Similarly, if you're a developer, there are free tools for pretty much any language you're likely to use; most famous is Eclipse for languages such as Java. But, even if you're a .NET developer, there are cost-free tools available for writing and compiling your programs.

In the general case, you're likely to be able to find cost-free options for at least part of the toolset you need, so you can spend your money only on the things you really need to.

LICENSING

If there's one factor that really makes the decision about moving to the cloud complicated, it's the minefield of software licensing. It's fair to say that software vendors don't make life easy for the benighted SMB owner.

For example, Microsoft offers Office 365 in a variety of forms, the licensing of which has changed since its launch. In February 2013, the company introduced a new licensing scheme for Office 365, providing different versions of the software. Rather confusingly, the company has also released a new version of its on-premise offering Office 2013

There are three basic versions of the software for small business:

- **Hosted email (Exchange Online) – this costs £2.60 per user per month**

- **Office 365 Small Business at £3.90 per user month**
- **Office 365 Small Business Premium £10.10 per user per month**

However, Microsoft is not alone in offering this level of complexity. Small businesses are continually faced with the problem of trying to make sense of software licensing. At least, they have it easier than large enterprises who are in a constant battle to ensure that they're not breaking their software suppliers' licensing conditions and, at the same time, ensuring they're not over-compensating.

On the other hand, businesses moving to IaaS implementation have it relatively easy. They're not going to be hit by unexpected charges, but moving from on-premise software to SaaS delivery, things can get a bit more complicated.

As it's unlikely that every supplier's licensing period will end at the same time, there will be a need to enter into a complex round of negotiations with the vendors. How successful this will be may partly depend on how well you are doing

Small businesses are continually faced with the problem of trying to make sense of software licensing.

as business – a supplier will be more inclined to cut you a deal if you're doing well – and may partly depend on the supplier's attitude to cloud. If it's a bit of a pioneer, it will be keen to introduce some cloud-friendly licensing.

CASH FLOW

One way in which cloud can help proceedings is by improving the way that cash flow is managed. The traditional way for small businesses to handle this is by using spreadsheets. This is not a perfect solution. It's hard to keep accurate tabs on income and outgoings but it's better than nothing.

It is a testament to the ongoing popularity of the spreadsheet (online and off) that if you Google 'cash flow' and 'spreadsheet' you will find all sorts of spreadsheet templates (many free, some not) designed to help

you manage cash flow. But, whilst this approach may be better than trying to do this manually, spreadsheets are not the most effective way to manage cash.

There are a number of cloud-based spreadsheets around that can help the small business keep better control. Microsoft's Office 365 of course, and its close competitor Google Apps are on offer, but there's also Zoho as an alternative. Such offerings have considerable advantages over their traditional counterparts; they can support more collaborative cash flow planning, and will make version control easier than juggling the numerous email attachments you might otherwise have to grapple with.

Companies that can predict their cashflow needs more accurately than their less well-performing peers are more likely to be doing this with the help of specialist software than with the general purpose spreadsheet, according to the Aberdeen Group.

The research also indicates that some types of specialist software are more effective than others. It finds that online tools for balance reporting, forecasting and account reconciliation (which can be provided by various types of software or service) are the 'technology enablers' that most effectively help organisations to predict their cash needs, even when fragmented financial functions and systems result in only partial views of cash.

> One of the ways in which cloud can help proceedings is by improving the way that cash flow is managed.

This is not so say that other specialist software and systems cannot be used to improve cash flow planning and cash management; they can. Many types of software that would once have been beyond the reach of small and medium-sized organisations (unless they had deep pockets) are now being made accessible and affordable by cloud-based specialists.

For example, Kyriba,

Reval and Treamo are among the organisations offering cloud-based treasury management systems that can be used to improve various aspects of cash analysis and management, and even achieve global cash management – something that was previously available only to the very largest multinationals with harmonised ERP systems and IT infrastructures, Adaptive Planning, Centage, and Host Analytics have also put systems into the hands of the many – for budgeting, planning and performance management.

Cloud-based software can also support a change in approach to managing cash flow. Setting periodic budgets, substituting actual figures from the management accounts on a month-by-month basis and then projecting future cash requirements, produces cash flow forecasts that are always out-of-date, incomplete and tend to be underestimates.

It is possible to get a real time view of cash commitments and more accurately predict requirements using 'commitment accounting', but until specialists such as Ariba, Compleat and Proactis, made cloud-based electronic procurement and spend

management software accessible and affordable, commitment accounting was too complex, time consuming and costly for most businesses to implement.

But it's not just about saving money by being more efficient. There are other ways in which cloud-based services can also cuts costs.

By using the right software, it's possible to consolidate corporate spend to nominated suppliers and by negotiating better prices and payment terms, small business can further reduce their overall spend.

So, in addition to helping you to manage your money much more

> **It's not just about saving money by being more efficient. There are other ways in which cloud-based services can also cut costs.**

efficiently cloud-based systems can give also you more cash to play with.

If there's one way to keep costs down, it's keeping a constant watch on what you're spending – as you're spending it. ■

■ CHAPTER 7 DOS AND DON'TS

Cloud best practice

Now you've decided you're ready to head in that upwardly direction, we run through the Dos and Don'ts of the cloud computing world...

BY NOW ANYONE LOOKING to move to cloud will feel they have a good idea of how to proceed. We hope you are satisfied you don't need the comfort of a dedicated IT department and that, at your fingertips, you can have enterprise-type computing.

It's not to say that cloud computing is the panacea for all computing problems and is not without its own problems. Most of all, you should be certain the cloud route is the one you want to go down; so do make certain it's the way you want to go.

You certainly need a decent networking connection so it's not for you if your broadband is insufficient.

One of the big dangers with cloud is the possibility of being stuck with one vendor and not being able to move data easily from one provider to another – you must always ensure there is an exit route.

And there are some other considerations too; if you have some development work done, you may find that the development platform is tied to particular cloud vendor – Salesforce and Force for example. The trend in the last 10 years has been to move towards more open computing, so make sure you're not tied to a proprietary offering.

Perhaps the most glaring point of all is cloud should be saving you money and, if it's not, it's a not a route you should be following.

It's obvious to state that keeping running costs to a minimum is a top priority for any business owner and that is the major reason why many are turning to pay-as-you-go web-based office products.

But, with so many companies and their products to choose from, picking the right one for you and your business can be tricky. With this in mind, we asked an assortment of technology industry experts for a list of dos and don'ts when it comes to choosing the right one.

DO TAKE TIME TO DECIDE WHAT SOFTWARE YOUR COMPANY NEEDS

Some new business owners may be tempted to sign up for lots of different software services before they've even bagged their first customer, lured – in part – by the relatively low monthly billing costs.

However, they may

> ## We hope you are satisfied you don't need the comfort of a dedicated IT department.

be better served by sticking to the business basics – such as web-based email and other office products – to start with as those bills will soon mount up.

Also, as Andy Burton, chairman of tech trade body the Cloud Industry Forum (CIF), points out, once your business is up and running, you may find the services you've signed up for are ill-suited to your needs.

"Take accountancy software, for example, if you've got a consulting business and are simply selling your time, you're not going to need a comprehensive suite of book-keeping software," Burton explains.

 ### DON'T SIGN UP WITHOUT RESEARCHING THE MARKET FIRST

You wouldn't enlist the services of a plumber or mechanic without asking for customer references first, and the same principle applies when scouting around for an online services provider.

Frank Jennings, a partner in the tech division at law firm DMH Stallard, explains: "It's very easy to set yourself up as a cloud services provider. I can buy a server off eBay, run some communications cables to it and run that as a business from my garage."

So, to ensure the one-man-band you're thinking of employing is worthy of your business, ask them to provide some accounts information, run a credit check on the company and ask around if anyone else has dealt with them, Jennings advises.

It is also worth quizzing the company about its future plans to see if it is planning to introduce or wind down features you might need.

 ### DO FIND OUT HOW EASY IT IS TO BREAK THE CONTRACT

Before you sign up with any online software provider, find out how easy it will be to get away from the contract, if you later find their services are not right for you.

For instance, how easy will it be to get your data back, will you have to pay a severance for breaking the

contract early, and how much help will you get moving your data elsewhere?

Stefan Töpfer, group CEO at Winweb Business Cloud, says users should avoid getting into long-term pay monthly contracts if possible.

"You should always have access to your data and be able to cancel at any time without any reason," he says.

Similarly, it is also worth bearing in mind that - if your provider goes out of business - the terms of your contract could become null and void.

"If the company directors are making you various promises, those are fine if the company is up and running, but as soon as it fails, the directors are not in charge anymore," warns Jennings.

DO HAVE A BACK-UP PLAN IN PLACE

Even the most high-profile online companies suffer downtime, and if you're planning to run your entire business from the cloud, you will need a backup plan to ensure your company can still operate.

CIF's Burton says most online service providers should have some resilience built in to protect customers in the event of an outage. Even so, it is also worth keeping a local copy of your data nearby.

"You can pick up a two terabyte

Do find out how easy it is to break the contract.

hard drive for £50 that plugs into your device so you can keep a physical local copy, as well as a cloud hosted one," Burton suggests.

"It is worth checking what kind of precautions an organisation has in place already [in case of an outage], but online storage should be the primary backup data store for a small business."

Meanwhile, Jennings points out that users should also consider signing up with multiple providers in order to protect themselves.

"If you've got a copy of the data on-premise, you can instruct another cloud provider to get you up and running again, but you should consider keeping a copy with another provider too," he offered.

"It will be another cost to consider, but - in the long run - it should make it easier to keep your business up and running".

DON'T FORGET TO QUIZ POTENTIAL PROVIDERS ABOUT DATA SECURITY

Entrusting your company data to an online firm takes a lot of trust, but there are steps you can take to ensure your (and customers') data is in safe hands.

Check if they hold any data security accreditations - such as the ISO 27001 certificate - or have affiliations with credible trade bodies, says Jennings.

"These things take time and money to achieve and if a provider has taken the trouble to acquire them, it should

What if it all goes wrong?

Plan for the worse case scenario: and in the case of out sourcing all your data storage to the cloud that means the cloud provider going under, going down or otherwise going AWOL and taking all your data with it.

The biggest hidden danger of the cloud is the notion that complete loss of data cannot occur. Unfortunately, the only failsafe solution is to retain a full data backup on your own servers or with a second remote provider. And that really negates the cost savings at the heart of cloud migration in the first place.

serve as a good indication of their commitment to the market," he says.

It is also worth finding out what software and appliances they use to safeguard data, and if they employ on-site security at their data centre.

"It really depends on how much the customer is looking to spend... because if they're talking about high risk data, that could put them out of business if they lost it, it might be worth bringing in a third party IT security expert to advise them on how best to approach the cloud."

 DO KEEP AN EYE ON YOUR EMPLOYEES

A small business, by its very definition will have few employees. But even in a small organisation, it's hard to keep tabs on employees.

As mentioned in the Security chapter of this guide, it's incredibly important to have a security policy that's adhered to in order to keep the systems running efficiently.

The problem with cloud is that one of its strengths is that it is easy for someone to download cloud software - unfortunately that also serves as one of its weaknesses.

In an ideal environment, the business manager/owner would take a measured view as to whether cloud computing is right for the business.

The danger is that some employees won't wait and find it all too easy to download consumer-type services, putting the business at risk: it doesn't take a genius to realise that the consumer cloud is no place for business data.

That said, don't think that blocking consumer services is enough: the manager/owner should also be wary of employees signing up to business-grade cloud services at this 'local' level, which could introduce platform incompatibilities or vendor lock-in

without you knowing.

 DON'T CONFUSE PLATFORM AND BUSINESS ARCHITECTURE

Most of the discussion around cloud has been concerned with technological change. It's not surprising: this entails a massive leap in the way that IT is handled but it's important to realise that moving to cloud isn't just about a new way to deliver software or a new way of hosting mission-critical platforms but could offer a new way to think about doing business.

Therefore, approach any change from a holistic business perspective which understands that 'how and where' are not as important as 'what

> **Even in a small organisation, it's good to keep tabs on employees.**

and why'. For example moving to a cloud-based platform could result in a change to working practices and a move to more flexible working.

This link between technology and the business needs to be at the forefront of all calculations. If a consultant comes in and recommends Amazon or Microsoft, for example, before properly auditing and understanding your core business needs then your migration into the cloud is likely to be a bit of a bumpy one.

 ### DO BE PATIENT WITH CLOUD

There's been plenty of hype about cloud computing and it will surely be the dominant technological platform in future but because it's relatively new it won't behave in the same way as more mature technologies.

Do remember, therefore, to be circumspect in your dealings. Do not entrust your mission critical website to a single server and host without some sort of contingency plan for unexpected downtime. Amazon suffered three major outages in little over a year. Any company without detailed recovery plans would have been in trouble.

Be wary of cloud providers too. Their systems are still immature at the moment and don't always perform accurately. It's not been unknown for providers to flag a perfectly innocent account as suspect and suspend it without any warning or contact.

 ### DON'T ASSUME YOUR DATA IS SECURE

It's tempting to think that if you've outsourced your data storage or application delivery to the cloud then you've outsourced the security of your data or application as well.

The truth is that if you've contracted with an infrastructure as a service (IaaS) model then security of your virtual servers will likely be mostly your responsibility.

It's not quite clear-cut: Platform-as-a-Service (PaaS) providers should shoulder more responsibility, but you need to be clear where the demarcation lines are drawn.

The boundary between IaaS and PaaS is becoming increasingly blurred and one provider will have different terms of service from another one.

When it comes to software as a service, there are different criteria to apply. You need to sort out ownership of data encryption keys. The Cloud Security Alliance (a body that provides guidance on cloud security issues) takes the view that organisations should weigh up the issues carefully.

The CSA points out that there are three options: holding the keys yourself, providing maximum security and availability; letting the SaaS vendor take control, this is cheaper but riskier; using the IaaS provider as a key-holder, you can be certain that the data will be encrypted but it does introduce an element of risk.

❌ DON'T FORGET THE SERVICE LEVEL AGREEMENT

SLAs are just as important in the cloud world as with any contracted service provider, so don't make the mistake of signing on the dotted line without first getting your lawyers to dot the Is and cross the Ts.

Do not skimp on legal advice, make sure that your lawyer has some knowledge of cloud services and has checked the details thoroughly.

Ensure that business-critical issues such as availability, security and responsibility are clearly covered in black and white. While a legally watertight SLA will not prevent cloud downtime, it will provide help with conflict resolution in the case of service interruption or downtime.

 DO REMEMBER IT'S A CASE OF SLOW, SLOW, NOT QUICK, SLOW

One thing you will probably not find in your cloud provider SLA is any mention of performance beyond uptime and availability expectations. If your applications have been developed with local data storage performance in mind, then don't be surprised if they falter somewhat courtesy of bandwidth and latency issues.

When researching cloud offerings, ensure that real world end-to-end performance at the I/O level has been factored into your analysis.

Speak to other customers and find out how they've been performing.

SLAs are as important in the cloud as with any contracted service provider.

Don't sign up for a long-term contract without monitoring the service.

If you want a quick check on current performance of the major providers have a look at Cloud Sleuth (www. cloudsleuth.net), this provides a real-time guide to how all major cloud providers are operating. You can also check individual servers: Amazon, for example, shows how all its data centres are currently performing. ■

■ **CHAPTER 8** CASE STUDIES

Avantifix CASE STUDY:1

This construction industry fixing solutions firm has embraced modern technologies to help make a good business even better...

ONE OF THE PROBLEMS facing any small firm is how much to invest in IT. After all, when you've got a turnover measured in thousands rather than millions, even the purchase of a server and some PCs may seem like a step too far.

Mike McElhatton, MD of Avantifix, a distributor of fixing solutions for the construction industry, was in that very position. Indeed, McElhatton, while appreciating the need for computers, is from the generation that's just as happy with pen and paper. "I have very little interest in IT, but it's part and parcel of the business," he says.

He didn't know how to progress with the IT system. "We had what I'd call a DIY system. We couldn't afford to have someone dedicated to IT but we could run what we had.

For example, would I be able to build a barbecue out of bricks, yes. Would I build a house, no? It would take 10 years," he says.

BACK THEN
Avantifix had a stock management system called Merlin– a DOS one no

ABOUT AVANTIFIX

Avantifix was founded in 1997.It is the largest Spit stockist in the UK, as well as supplying a wide range of other big and smaller name products to its customer base.
■ www.avantifix.co.uk

I have very little interest in IT, but it's part and parcel of the business.

less, hosted on Windows 2003 server, which was clearly coming to the end of its natural life. The company did have a website but it didn't enable customers to make purchases on account. And, for a firm that makes most of its sales to account customers, billing them later, this was a serious omission. McElhatton realised the system had to be upgraded but didn't really know how to proceed. The replacement of the company's financial controller turned out to be the key to the process as that led to the introduction of a new service provider, i-Virtuals.

Ashoka Reddy, i-Virtuals managing director quickly ascertained that Avantifix would be a perfect candidate for a cloud-based system: the company had little or no internal IT expertise and was in urgent need of a more flexible infrastructure.

However, McElhatton was also concerned that the company was not being pushed down a path of buying more than it actually needed. "It's like the old-style Nokia phone. That was perfect for just making phone calls: it just worked. A computer system doesn't need to have any more than we need doing."

MAKING WAY FOR CHANGE

The internal system has been moved to an i-Virtuals cloud, with the on-premise server being used as backup to provide added resilience. That is a new departure for the company. In the past, they didn't get backed up but, drawing on one of the advantages of the cloud, everything is now backed up automatically.

The new system allows Avantifix to run a network of 10 PCs, providing access to the Merlin stock control system and Sage accounting. The company also uses the system to connect employees' iPads.

The new system means Avantifix can stay on top of software licensing.

One step that Avantifix is still to deal with is the issue of its website. While there's an acceptance that it needs upgrading, there is the thorny problem of bringing together information from a variety of different sources, all of which have their own individual formats.

Reddy says upgrading the website would mean developing a completely integrated system that's linked to the same database - that would be very time-consuming to implement.

As McElhatton explains this would be something only he and his team could do as it's a task that requires human involvement.

REALISING REAL BUSINESS BENEFITS TODAY AND TOMORROW

The website is being moved incrementally ready for the wholesale deployment later in 2013. The i-Virtuals cloud is hosted in a data centre in Manchester. Reddy has rejected the idea of using an established cloud provider such as Amazon or Microsoft because he wanted ready access to the servers. "It's important to have customer data

> ### ■ AT A GLANCE:
> # What happened?
>
> Avantifix is a company with little IT expertise in-house. By talking to a local provider, it managed to move most of its applications to the cloud.
>
> It is now set to transfer the rest of its app estate to the cloud later this year. As a result, it runs its IT more cost effectively while at the same time enhancing security.

held in the UK," says Reddy.

While using a third-party provider could have proved problematical, McElhatton says it hasn't worked that way.

He doesn't think of Reddy as a supplier but as a valued member of the team. "He's added a lot to the business. I feel that I can trust him to do the right thing for us and that kind of trust doesn't happen overnight," he says. There's the financial imperative too. "Having him around can save us money," adds McElhatton.

A company that had little in the way of IT infrastructure and skills in-house can now run a range of apps and is in the process of developing a website that will match its competitors' offerings. It's run on a mixture of (limited) internal know-how and external expertise – the best of both worlds. ■

BETE

CASE STUDY:2

As a unique company, BETE required a solution that met its individual needs. And, the beauty of the cloud, is that's more than possible, quickly and easily...

THERE'S BEEN A RADICAL change in the way that many companies conduct their business in the last decade or so. There are now a growing number of firms who choose not to have a central office and where employees work elsewhere.

BETE, a distributor of industrial spray nozzles and other fluid handling components, is one such example. The company employs eight staff and has an annual turnover of more than £1 million, yet –excluding its warehouse – it does not have a central business premises. Indeed, all staff work from home.

The money saved from renting business premises can instead be ploughed back into the business, giving the company a major cash flow advantage at a time when many small firms are struggling to keep their heads above water. In fact, BETE has made it one of the defining characteristics of its business.

BUSINESS-CRITICAL BUSINESS PRACTICES

BETE's business model entirely depends on ensuring that its employees have ultra-reliable access to critical business applications and data. Until 2011, the corporate network consisted of servers hosted in a co-location centre, which employees accessed over a Virtual Private Network (VPN) that was run over twin ADSL connections: one for voice communications, the other for data.

BETE had some serious concerns about a service that relied on two separate providers, as the company's marketing manager, Ivan Zytynski, explains.

"When you rely on the internet for every aspect of business operations, reliability is paramount," said Zytynski. "When you have two providers, one for the internet connection and the other in charge of the hosting, there is

ABOUT BETE

BETE is a leader in its field distributing standard and custom-made spray solutions for various applications and industries. It prides itself on order efficiency and customer service and support.

■ www.bete.co.uk

an inevitable lack of accountability for overall service availability. If the network goes down it's pretty much impossible for the customer to pinpoint what's gone wrong between the hosting and network providers."

There was an additional concern too, the lack of flexibility. The company used its own servers hosted in the co-lo centre, if the company wanted to expand, it needed to buy additional servers. On top of that, each employee needed a dedicated ADSL line and firewall.

BETE approached its network provider Claranet to implement an integrated hosting and network service to keep employees connected to critical data and LOB applications.

Claranet proposed its Virtual Data Centre (VDC) service, its

> When you rely on the internet for every aspect of business operations, reliability is paramount.

Infrastructure-as-a-Service (IaaS) offering, enabling users to provision virtual compute, storage and networking resources in one click. The VDC allows BETE to host its line of business applications in a virtualised environment, with most of BETE's infrastructure migrated from physical servers to virtual machines. Claranet takes responsibility for managing the infrastructure, as well as optimising the performance of the applications.

Claranet's VDC holds the customer relationship management (CRM) system, stock control software and e-marketing applications. It also holds BETE's remote desktop services (RDS), which is critical for enabling remote-working staff to access applications and data over the network. It also provides BETE with a "burst" capacity of extra RAM for periods of high demand.

CHANGE FOR THE BETTER

The old ADSL lines connecting employees' homes to the network were removed. The company now uses Claranet's own MPLS backbone which does not touch the public internet. It also ensures BETE only has one provider responsible for service availability – a critical consideration when one entrusts the entire business to the cloud.

"The money that we save on renting, heating and running an office means that we can invest in the very best IT and networking services on the market," says Zytynski. "When your business utterly relies on service availability, as ours does, you simply can't compromise by using anything but the best."

Since moving home working employees have experienced near-total availability says Zytynski.

"Moving our applications into a virtualised environment has given us the flexibility that we need to meet changing demand quickly without the need to purchase expensive physical servers," continues Zytynski. "If we want to deploy a new app, for example, we don't have to worry about whether our current servers can handle it, as we can simply upgrade the allocated RAM."

The company also benefits from moving to an MPLS backbone. Zytynski says that the company has saved budget on security and network management.

The BETE experience is testament to the power of the cloud and the flexibility it can provide to employees. "At BETE, we want to run a company that really is different from others; where staff can enjoy working from their own homes, and to their own flexible timetables. While some firms might be scared of home working, our employees have all responded wonderfully to the trust that we have placed in them, says Zytynski. ■

■ AT A GLANCE:
What happened?

BETE is a company without an office let alone an IT department.

Its employees work from their homes thanks to an IaaS implementation from its provider, Claranet. It shows that you definitely don't need fancy headquarters in order to run a succesful company.

Telegraph Hill

Telegraph Hill is a modern company with modern needs, deploying modern technologies to provide real business advantage.

TELEGRAPH HILL IS A company for the modern age. It's the sort of firm that would never have existed 10 years ago. In fact, it wouldn't have even been dreamt about. It has emerged from the interface between several concepts: the rise of digital media, the importance of social networking and the commoditisation of video and production equipment. In particular, it's a company that's a walking embodiment of the move away from creative silos, where people are pigeonholed into a particular skill set.

As the company boasts on its website "We are proud to be multi-skilled. We shoot, cut, code, grade, paint, plan, process, present, discuss, design, decide and do. Daily". The company has been working with some well-known TV programmes such as Merlin and The Voice, and in March also launched a programme, The Fox Problem, that appeared solely on You Tube.

Its founders, Garret Keogh, Barry Pilling and Jack Simcock, have a background in TV production and are well used to this multidisciplinary approach.

NEW AGE COMPANY, NEW AGE TECHNIQUES

The company launched at the end of 2011 and just as the concept for the company couldn't have existed 10 years earlier, operationally it couldn't have existed 10 years earlier either. Most start-ups operate by finding a premises and building from there, but Telegraph Hill, in the early stages, at least, operated without a head office and relied almost entirely on cloud technology. The company used Skype for conferences and phone calls, it kept files on Dropbox, and used Gmail

ABOUT TELEGRAPH HILL

Telegraph Hill likes to make, share and talk. The company produces compelling content and live events and then shares those creations via digital platforms as well as engaging its audience and building long-term relationships through social media networks.
■ http://wearetelegraphhill.com/

> ## What first seemed exciting and innovative just became a massive pain...

and Google Calendar. Naturally, as would be expected from a creative organisation, the founders already had Macbooks and iPhones.

For a time, the company didn't even have a central office. "We were very proud of being a new type company that worked in the cloud and didn't really have an office. Our teams worked in the client's space or on-set so we could work wherever we wanted. I used a shared workspace called The Hub in Kings Cross for a while. The three of us caught up via Skype or a Google Hangouts or occasionally Facetime," says Keogh. But that approach to communication couldn't last.

"What first seemed exciting and innovative just became a massive pain," he adds. Some friends offered us to sublet a floor of the Perseverance Works in Shoreditch. We're now about to take over the whole space as the team has grown so quickly."

EMBRACING THE CLOUD

The company may have had a change in approach to physical workspace but is still very much a user of cloud services. "Our main business communications apps are via Google Apps for Business – we use mail and calendars mainly. It's great for easily adding new staff and setting up new accounts," says Keogh.

It's an approach that's helped with the fast growth of the company. "We quickly grew from three people to 16 now and each new member of staff can be set up in minutes." For storage, the company stores all its files on Dropbox. "I try to discourage staff from keeping anything locally on their hard disks," says Keogh. "Although we have upgraded to Dropbox for Teams as the company expanded."

Cloud plays its part throughout the company. "Accounts are all done via Quickbooks Online which our accountants also have access to. We enter everything in here from invoices and payments to receipts and tax info. It automatically sends invoices to our clients for us and makes end of year financial returns easier," says Keogh. "We work with an external payroll company (Ceridian) for the core payroll work and use WeTransfer for sending big files and Vimeo is where we store viewing copies of all our videos for client sign off."

The company used to base everything in the cloud but it has branched out since those early days.

"We only recently set up a small network based around Mac Minis. This is used by the editing team who used to work off external hard drives – this was unmanageable. We now have a proper backup system in place which is often contractually required by our clients when we're handling important video footage" he says. The new Mac Mini network was the first time the company had actually spent money in setting up their systems.

TECH SAVVY

The company operates without any IT staff, but it does contain an above-average level of computer expertise.

Keogh has an approach to sourcing kit that other firms would find hard to follow. "When a new starter joins, I'm usually the one who heads down to the Apple Store to buy their computer and set them up. It's kind of fun to walk into the Apple and buy some cool new kit from the office. Obviously this isn't scalable but at the moment I'm happy to oversee IT purchases and strategy until we grow further."

Telegraph Hill is a new sort of company based around flexibility of hours and location. It's a process made easier by technology. Even the move towards a central office reflects this as Keogh explains.

"The physical office space is really important. Everything then becomes a part of the culture of the company: from the pictures on the wall, the music on the stereo or the drinks in the fridge. We spend a lot of time at work so it may as well be as nice a place as possible."

Maybe not a sentiment you'd have heard about workplaces 20 years ago, but a sign of the times. ∎

■ AT A GLANCE:
What happened?

Telegraph Hill is a media start-up that needs no IT department.

Its team of skilled professionals operates a range of media applications using in-house machines coupled with cloud-based software for running the company.

Freedom to focus on what matters to your business

Sage 200: More choice, more freedom

Slick Machine provides administration and financial services to companies who prefer to outsource this kind of work. Business has grown rapidly with a turnover of £24 million in 2012, up by 30% from the previous year. And their customers demand high levels of service.

They turned to Sage 200 to help them deal with the thousands of transactions, statements and banking functions they manage for their customers every day and improve efficiency by automating many of their manual processes.

"Contracts require us to perform to a certain service level," Darren Reynolds, Director of Slick Machine explains, "That means 99% of payments received before noon must be directly allocated by 2:00pm the same day."

Sage 200 helps companies manage their finances, customers and gain business insight all in one solution. It's designed to help different departments work together efficiently, by sharing data and delivering real cost benefits.

As director of the business, Darren can see for himself how Sage 200 is helping streamline their processes. "I can log in every day and see our account data and record transactions," he explains. "And I can do that from anywhere with the software installed on my PC. I don't have to worry about the back end at all."

Being able to work freely and flexibly is important to Slick Machine, and they need a solution that doesn't mean a big investment in IT infrastructure and support.

So, new cloud-based, Sage 200 Online, is ideal. It's built on the Windows® Azure™ platform, making it secure, resilient and highly scalable as business grows.

"When I take on a new customer, I don't have anything to worry about," says Darren. "I don't have to go and buy a load of new servers. I don't have to worry about installing operating systems, server software and set up. I don't have to do any of that."

Sage 200 Online integrates with in-house software and online banking systems to help Slick Machine deal with multiple customers and transactions smoothly. It means they can take advantage of new opportunities without the cost and headache of investing heavily in IT systems and support.

"There's a great market opportunity if we can hone our skills and use the best technology to handle business processes more accurately and efficiently than other companies," Darren says.

By using Sage 200 to streamline their business, they can focus on their core services. "We can get someone up to speed on a particular task in a couple of minutes," says Darren. "I don't ask when I'm recruiting people about their software experience. I'm more interested in their customer service and general financial skills."

Slick Machine's business relies on them providing better financial and administration services than other companies can manage in house. They benefit from the same kind of relationship with their software suppliers.

"I've always felt that as a strong and reputable brand in the marketplace, Sage has the resources to be able to deliver a stable solution that's well-tested by a large number of other customers," Darren says.

"The professionals at Sage and their partners are more capable of maintaining availability and reliability than any technicians I could hire in my business."

I'm not interested in wires and service packs. I'm not interested in upgrades or any of that. I've got a business to run."
Darren Reynolds, Director, Slick Machine.

....

For more information:
www.sage.co.uk/sage-200 | Tel: 0845 111 9988 | Email: customer.development@sage.com

■ CHAPTER 9 HEALTHCHECK

Cloud Healthcheck

How do you know that you're ready to move to the cloud? What steps should you be taking to prepare yourself? What are the danger points?

LARGE CORPORATES ARE FOND of cloud readiness assessments. These are usually long questionnaires, devised to draw out the state of an enterprise's existing systems. There's a degree of complexity in bringing cloud to a larger business – a problem that SMBs don't have to contend with.

That's not to say small businesses can be blasé about the difficulties of using cloud services – there are still other factors to consider. There's no right way or wrong way to move to the cloud but there are some basic questions to ask yourself.

1 WHAT SKILL LEVELS DO YOU HAVE IN YOUR BUSINESS?

One of the big advantages of moving to the cloud is the lack of requirement for an IT department – hence the title of this book – but it's not really for someone who has no skills at all. There may well be some elementary configuration to do – and you'll certainly need to do some rudimentary connectivity.

2 DO YOU HAVE A RELIABLE BROADBAND SERVICE?

To run cloud services, you need a reliable connection. If you're in the middle of nowhere with a basic modem, it's not going to work. The basic premise of cloud is that services are delivered online so if you haven't got that, there's little point in proceeding.

3 HOW SENSITIVE IS YOUR DATA?

What personal information are you handling? How secure does your set-up have to be? Are you taking any risks in holding it? Will using the cloud increase or decrease those risks? Remember, contrary to popular wisdom, cloud will not always be a riskier option: personal information held on an insecure machine sitting under a desk in your office could be considerably more vulnerable than being held by a cloud

There's a degree of complexity in bringing cloud to larger enterprises – a problem SMBs don't have to contend with.

services provider, who may well have comprehensive security policies.

4 DO YOU REALLY KNOW YOUR PROVIDER?

If you're entrusting your data to a cloud services provider, it's essential to be totally happy with that company. Does it have a reputation for poor service? Has it had security breaches in the past? It's worth conducting a search for words such as "breach." It's important to note that a security breach in itself is not a problem, just as long as it's tightened up procedures since then. Check forums for customer

comments – try to get a feeling for what the provider is like.

5 WHAT ARE THE CONTRACT TERMS?

Do you know where your data is being held? Will you be able to get it out of the service provider if needs be? What will happen if the provider goes bust? What are the terms for reliability of service – if the cloud server goes down, will you be left high and dry? Do make sure that a lawyer has read the contract and you are aware of your rights.

6 WHAT ARE YOUR EMPLOYEES LIKE?

Employees can be the weak link in any organisation. By moving to the cloud, you could be increasing your level of risk: are your employees

> **If you're entrusting your data to a cloud services provider, it's essential to be totally happy with that.**

aware of the security implications of moving to the cloud? Are they liable to bring in their own devices, thus compromising your security? Before moving to the cloud, you should implement a security policy and ensure it's adhered to. This could include forbidding consumer applications like iTunes or Facebook – although both of these could have business uses so don't get too heavy-handed.

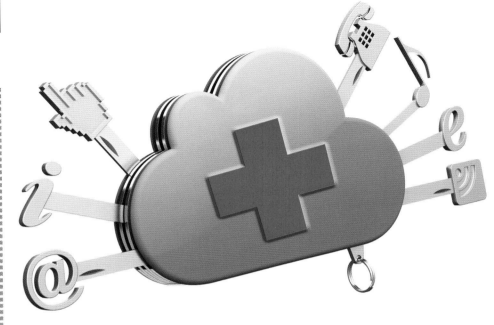

Are your employees aware of the security implications of moving to the cloud?

There's also the issue of compatibility to overcome.

7 SOFTWARE LICENSING

This could be a minefield. Do check the current status of your software licences and ensure that you're not paying for the same products twice.

8 LEGACY SOFTWARE

If you have a large amount of customised software that keeps your business ticking over, cloud may not be the right choice for you – remember the adage, "if it ain't broke, don't fix it". Software like that may not be the easiest to move to the cloud.

9 COMPLIANCE

If you work in a regulated industry, you have to be wary of how your compliance guidelines are to be enforced by a cloud provider.

10 CHANGE IN YOUR OUTLOOK

Moving to the cloud requires a completely different business philosophy. It changes the way you use technology and it could change the way that you work as you will no longer be confined to the office. It will certainly change your approach to security and will lead to a new way of thinking about costs. It's a move that could shake-up your business but needs careful thought beforehand. ∎

Glossary

AUTHENTICATION

The computer term for confirming the identity of an individual. It is particularly important in cloud computing set-ups where there's a need to ensure that individuals are who they say they are.

AMAZON WEB SERVICES (AWS)

The name given to the Amazon subsidiary that provides a public cloud service. It offers a variety of different cloud services, including EC2 – its IaaS service and S3, its cloud storage offering. AWS is known for its ease of purchasing but has also a reputation of providing little help for the user.

AZURE (SEE WINDOWS AZURE)

CapEx

Stands for Capital Expenditure and is the traditional way to purchase IT equipment. Large investments are made in one financial year to benefit the business over the lifetime of the hardware which would typically be three to five years. This is in contrast to OpEx.

CLOUD BACKUP

Backing up data to internet-based storage systems.

As well as being a simple way to back up data it has the added benefit of keeping a copy of data offsite. Disadvantages can potentially include the amount of time to backup and restore files, particularly where data changes frequently and internet bandwidth is limited.

CLOUD INFRASTRUCTURE

This consists of servers, Storage Area Networks (SANs), networking components and virtualisation software that combine to provide a fault tolerant, flexible and scalable system. Cloud infrastructures are housed in data centres.

CLOUD SERVICE PROVIDER

A company that provides cloud services over the internet. Large data centres are used to run applications and store data in fault tolerant configurations. The long list of providers includes Amazon, Google, Microsoft and Salesforce.com.

CLOUD STORAGE

Storage of files on internet based systems. Cloud storage can be used as part of a SaaS offering where the application and storage are both located on the cloud. Another option is to use it to store data that can be transferred to or from the local network via a web browser or locally installed application. Companies offering cloud storage solutions include Amazon, Rackspace and Microsoft.

CUSTOMER RELATIONSHIP MANAGEMENT (CRM)

Software that enables sales professionals to keep tabs on customers by providing a more accurate method of keeping records. The cloud CRM market is dominated by Salesforce.com

DATA CENTRE

Buildings that house cloud infrastructures including servers, storage systems and networking equipment. They are also known as cloud centres.

ENTERPRISE RESOURCE PLANNING (ERP)

A software suite that provides a way of integrating different enterprise apps under one framework. Typically it will cover accounting, stock control, sales (CRM) and other similar products. It's increasingly being used by smaller companies to automate many of their processes.

GOOGLE APPS

The name given to Google's office productivity suite, a competitor to Microsoft Office 365. Google Apps comprises Google Docs, Gmail,

Calendar, Sheets (spreadsheet software) and access to Google Drive storage

HYBRID CLOUD

A system that uses a combination of private and public clouds – these can be from one provider or a multitude of different vendors.

INFRASTRUCTURE AS A SERVICE (IAAS)

Service that provides access to virtual servers. In the case of a public cloud, this service would be hosted by a third party and accessed over the internet. It's important to be aware of licensing implications when using this type of service. Services are normally billed on the consumption of resources such as processor and memory. Amazon and Rackspace both offer services in this area.

MULTI-TENANCY

A single instance of an application used for many customers, with each customer only able to access their own data. Customers may be able to customise aspects of the software for their data, but only within the limitations imposed by the developers.

OpEx

Stands for Operational Expenditure with costs incurred for services within a financial year. As cloud computing is charged on a subscription basis, it marks a shift from CapEx to OpEx, making budgeting easier.

PLATFORM AS A SERVICE (PAAS)

Service that provides a framework for developers to run their own code and so can be used for in-house applications. This service is particularly useful when SaaS solutions don't meet the particular business needs. The publishing of applications can be greatly speeded up by using this type of service as the hardware and required components are set up by the provider. Services like Force.com and Microsoft's Windows Azure fit into this category.

PRIVATE CLOUD

Using virtualisation technology to provide similar functionality to a public cloud, but owned and managed by a single company. Private clouds may be more suitable than a public cloud when highly sensitive information is stored. The large hardware manufacturers such as Cisco, Dell, HP and IBM provide hardware tailored for private clouds.

PUBLIC CLOUD

Cloud services provided across the internet by third-party providers. Virtualisation technology is used to provide fault tolerant, flexible and expandable systems that can be divided to provide isolated services on a subscription or usage basis. Companies providing services include Amazon, Google, Microsoft and Salesforce.com.

SALESFORCE.COM

One of the prime movers towards the whole concept of cloud computing. Made a name for itself by delivering software online, using SaaS technology. The company started by offering CRM applications – aiming them at non-techie staff. It has expanded to other apps since then.

STORAGE AREA NETWORK (SAN)

Large fault tolerant storage system that can be accessed through technologies such as fibre channel or iSCSI to provide storage to multiple servers.

SANs work with virtualisation technology, enabling virtual servers to be moved between physical servers on-the-fly.

SOFTWARE AS A SERVICE (SAAS)

Software delivered to customers via the internet. It is usually seen as including office applications, email services and CRM systems. The hardware and software is managed by the provider, so there is little requirement for local IT staff for this type of service. SaaS products are paid for on a subscription basis.

SERVICE LEVEL AGREEMENT (SLA)

This defines the level of service that a supplier will provide, normally including the percentage of uptime and levels of compensation offered if the supplier doesn't meet expectations.

UTILITY COMPUTING

Providing computing services and charging on a usage basis in much the same way that electricity is charged. This is a shift from traditional networks where servers need to be purchased and then replaced on a schedule.

VIRTUALISATION

Technology used for cloud computing that divides physical servers into multiple smaller virtual servers each containing their own fully functioning operating system. Virtual servers can be migrated between physical servers and resources such as processor and memory can be increased or decreased as required. Citrix, Microsoft and VMware provide virtualisation solutions.

VOICE OVER IP

A system that enables telephony over a computer network (IP being the name given to the protocol that underlies the internet – it stands for Internet Protocol). The most widely-used VoIP service is Skype but there are a variety of enterprise-strength alternatives.

WINDOWS AZURE

This is Microsoft's own cloud platform. It offers close integration with other Microsoft products, particularly the Hyper-V virtualisation offering and Windows Server 2012. Windows Azure is both an IaaS and a PaaS product. ■